PASTA FRESCA

Also by Viana La Place and Evan Kleiman
CUCINA FRESCA

PASTA FRESCA

Viana La Place
AND
Evan Kleiman

Illustrations by Ann Field

WILLIAM MORROW
AND COMPANY, INC.
New York

TO MICHELE AND JIM

Library of Congress Cataloging-in-Publication Data
La Place, Viana.
  Pasta fresca.

  Bibliography: p.
  Includes index.
  1. Cookery (Macaroni)   I. Kleiman, Evan.   II. Title.
TX809.M17L34 1988   641.8'22   88-9294
ISBN 0-688-07763-3

Printed in the United States of America

First Edition

1 2 3 4 5 6 7 8 9 10

BOOK DESIGN BY RICHARD ORIOLO

ACKNOWLEDGMENTS

Food is the central theme of our lives. We spend hours thinking, reading, and talking about it in one guise or another with friends, family, and colleagues. We are indebted to all who participate with us in this informal process of learning and professional growth, for all "new" ideas are a synthesis of what has come before. For their inspiration and mentorship we want to thank Elizabeth David, Marcella Hazan, Giuliano Bugialli, and Ada Boni, who were the first among many teachers.

There are those we want to thank individually. Our agents, Maureen and Eric Lasher, worked hard to see this project finally come together. Thanks to Kathy Ternay for her help in testing some of the recipes.

Evan would like to thank John and Carla Strobel, the staffs of Angeli Caffe and Trattoria Angeli, and her steadfast assistant, Eadie Kleiman, for their support and patience during the writing of this book.

Viana would like to thank Rachel Dourec of Montana Mercantile for being so supportive. She gives loving thanks to her parents, Pierre and Antonietta La Place, for the sharing of culture and ideas which became a part of this book.

CONTENTS

PASTA FRESCA

INTRODUCTION

*P*asta Fresca, like our first book, *Cucina Fresca,* is a reflection of our personal tastes. Although *pasta fresca,* translated from the Italian, refers to egg pasta made at home, we have taken poetic license in using it to express our style of making pasta dishes using both fresh and dried pasta. *Pasta Fresca,* to us, means pasta that is fresh, vivid, and uncomplicated.

We both grew up in southern California, a place of intense sun, warm Santa Ana breezes, and gentle hills covered with wild fennel and prickly pear cactus. The Pacific Ocean always beckoned. Citrus groves and avocado orchards were only a few feet away, and the trees were somehow always heavy with fruit. California's long growing season made us take for granted the abundance of vegetables and fruits, their low cost and freshness. This endless summer called for a way of eating that was naturally lighter and better suited to simplicity. Trips to Italy to visit family and friends followed, opening up a whole new world where meals are important daily rituals, and where there is a deep respect for the traditions of eating that goes back centuries. In landscape and climate, Italy mirrors California, and we began to make connections between the two. We were awed by the deeply rooted cultural beauty found not only in towering cathedrals but in the small details of a village bread shop. A different path led each of us to Italy, but once there we felt strongly and irrevocably connected to it. *Pasta Fresca* is a collection of recipes that reflects a combining of our memories and impressions.

This is not a book about pasta and sauces as separate elements. They must be seen together as complete dishes. Each sauce relates to its paired pasta shape in an integral way. It is very important to remember that when we speak of sauces we are not just referring to a smooth-textured liquid that coats the pasta — such as a blend of tomato, herbs, and olive oil or a mixture of Gorgonzola and cream — a sauce can also be just fresh peas and butter or sautéed bits of artichoke and pancetta. In keeping with our philosophy of simplicity, most of the sauces in this book can be prepared in about the time it takes to boil water for the pasta.

To us, *Pasta Fresca* means dishes made with ripe, red tomatoes, quickly cooked over a hot flame to keep them sweet, with fresh basil as bright green and fragrant as just-picked herbs from the garden. *Pasta Fresca* means a sauce that is as simple as lemon juice and raw tomatoes, bathed in aromatic olive oil. Vegetables of all kinds — artichokes, fennel, tender asparagus, sweet peppers, zucchini — become sauces. Cheeses, from goat cheese to smoked mozzarella, are quickly transformed into satisfying dishes when matched with pasta. The flavors of fresh tuna, pink shrimp, and little clams full of briny juices are allowed to shine through unencumbered. For cold nights when a comforting dish of pasta is called for, we eat rustic dishes carefully prepared with beef, or tiny veal meatballs, combined with mild ricotta or tangy provolone, and cooked with the best imported Italian canned tomatoes and sweet aromatic vegetables.

It is this respect and love for the ingredients themselves that keep the food direct and keep the eating experience pure. Although we do include the more complex stuffed and baked pastas, there is an underlying simplicity at work.

Pasta Fresca includes recipes based on all we know about Italian food. Some take off in a slightly new direction, but we think they will have lasting appeal. Many are regional Italian recipes that we love and eat all the time. In creating new recipes we always try to keep true to our food sense.

Pasta is no longer considered just a *primo piatto,* a first course. It can be a quick and satisfying lunch as well as the focus of an artful and sophisticated dinner. We see our recipes as being a guide to relaxed, fun eating that expresses a sense of freedom. Pasta has come to symbolize all that is fresh and spontaneous about the way we eat today. It is more than just an ethnic food, set apart from everyday eating. It is embraced by everyone for its comforting qualities, ease of preparation, healthfulness, and magical ability to tap into our communal and individual fantasy of Italy. It is a loving offering for friends and family, or a joyful meal for one. In its golden contours can be found an unending supply of honest food that nourishes and delights us.

La Guida

A Guide to Pasta

*P*asta is a food that has always transcended boundaries. It has been eaten passionately, by the poor as well as by the aristocracy. It is eaten by the people of southern Italy as well as by northerners. It is an everyday food and it is a food for celebrations. For Italians, pasta is part of the ritual of daily life that unfolds around the dinner table. It is at the table that one's need for sustenance transforms itself into shared pleasure. Often at the center of that table is an abundance of golden, glowing pasta.

When the first wave of Italian immigrants arrived on these shores, they brought with them their love for pasta. Unfortunately, when it came to the kind of food that ended up being labeled "Italian" in restaurants, it bore little resemblance to the authentic Italian kitchen. Vaguely Neapolitan in origin, it was an attempt to re-create dishes from memories of meals prepared by the mothers and sisters of those early Italian immigrants. The ingredients were at times of poor quality and, often, necessary ones were unavailable, leading to some dreadful substitutions.

Soon the spaghetti house became a fixture of many American towns. The pasta served in these restaurants was overcooked and drowned in strong, bitter tomato sauces that had been on the stove since time immemorial, with gigantic meatballs perched precariously on top of the pasta. This image was so firmly planted in the American mind that changing it has been, and sometimes continues to be, an uphill struggle. In an attempt to change direction, Italian food in America went from its pseudo-Neapolitan beginnings of frighteningly brown tomato sauce on pale strands of soft spaghetti to a so-called "northern cuisine" with rubbery fresh pasta served in a pool of heavily reduced cream. What these misguided efforts had in common was a lack of understanding of the true style of Italian cooking and how it relates to pasta. This history of poorly made Italian food led to a misconception that it is heavy. It is now commonly accepted by doctors and others in the health community that a diet consisting of good pasta, fresh vegetables, seafood, and fine olive oil is one of the healthiest and lightest ways of eating. Years ago it was simply what the land and the economy would yield.

Pasta Shapes

Over the years pasta has come to embody the spirit of the Italian people — inventive, fanciful, resourceful, full of fun and charm. Even in the face of adversity, the Italians' genuine love of artistry and their natural creativity produced from flour and water a myriad of pasta shapes as beautiful as tiny sculptures. Although meals for many poor families consisted mostly of pasta, the variety of shapes and the way they were combined with other ingredients produced dishes that not only looked very different, but felt and tasted very different. In this way, pasta not only satisfied hunger in the belly, but in its diversity, satisfied the need for variety. The various shapes were not only artful, but cleverly designed to best serve the needs of the sauce. The shapes reflect a gentle, playful sensibility in tune with nature — representing little tongues, tiny thimbles, fine hair, large ribbons, stars, large snails, and little butterflies. Recent additions to the catalog of shapes include representations of radiators and car-door handles, a wry and funny commentary on modern Italy.

Over the years strict formulas were developed by the Italians, who pay serious attention to the guidelines governing what pasta shape to use with what sauce. These rules have been handed down from generation to generation and are to be respected. They are the results of centuries of learning about and understanding the properties of each shape in relation to the sauce. For example, when you use dried pasta, the very thin, long type goes well with soupy shellfish sauces because it absorbs the juices without becoming soft. Tubular shapes are perfect for trapping bits of vegetables or meats. The stronger, more assertively flavored sauces match the more pronounced flavor of thicker pasta. Fresh pasta shapes, usually long and flat, go best with delicate sauces, cream and butter, ingredients that can be absorbed by the extremely porous surface of the dough.

While pasta has a long history rooted firmly in the ancient past, like Italy itself pasta refuses to live in the past. Rules pertaining to sauces and the proper pasta shapes do not mean that there is no room for fantasy. It will be the proverbial test of time that determines whether these new sauces are passing fads or whether, under serious scrutiny by grandmothers and mothers all over Italy, they will be accepted into the fold.

The Truth About Fresh and Dried Pasta

Although people are becoming more sophisticated about true Italian food, there is one major misconception that has arisen out of the attempt to upgrade Italian food in America. The confusion revolves around the issue of fresh versus dried pasta. In the minds of many people, fresh homemade pasta is superior and dried pasta is an inferior substitute. *The truth is that both fresh pasta and dried pasta are equally good. Fresh pasta, made properly, and high-quality imported dried pasta are used for different reasons. Neither is superior to the other.* There are many factors that go into determining when each should be used. The illustrated pasta shapes (see pages 22–26 and 28–30) will help guide you in making the proper choices of pasta and sauce. Understanding this concept of different but equal is crucial. It is at the heart of this book. A dish of imported factory-made spaghetti with a tomato and eggplant sauce is just as much a cause for celebration as a dish of fresh fettuccine with butter and Parmesan cheese. As a matter of fact, today, all over Italy, dried pasta is eaten much more often than fresh because of its flavor, texture, and convenience.

Dried Pasta

Pasta secca, or "dried pasta," is made from pale golden-yellow durum wheat, also referred to as hard wheat or semolina, and water. It is a dough that has traditionally been manufactured industrially. Through the years, Italians have developed sophisticated techniques to produce the finest dried pasta — the quality of water, the blend of hard-wheat flour used, the dies used to extrude the dough, and the drying procedures have all been important factors.

Because of its lightly nutty flavor, dried pasta is usually matched with olive oil–based sauces, with chunky meats, vegetables, and cheeses, as well as with sauces that contain red chile pepper or other strong flavorings. It is also used with all kinds of tomato sauces. Because of dried pasta's compact texture, it has the distinct advantage of being able to absorb water and swell in size while remaining al dente. All the imported Italian pasta brands are good. We particularly recommend the De Cecco brand. It stays al dente longer once cooked, has a strong texture and fine flavor, and doesn't split while cooking.

Dried Pasta Shapes

anellini — *little rings*

cavatelli — *little hollowed-out shapes*

elbows

conchigliette — *little shells*

Small Shapes for Soup — small, delicate shapes in clear beef broth, chicken broth, light vegetable soups; larger shapes in rustic soups with beans or assorted vegetables

capellini — *fine hairs*

spaghetti — *little strings (broken into shorter lengths)*

Long, Thin Strands for Soup — very thin strands in clear broths and light vegetable soups; slightly thicker ones in vegetable soups and bean soups

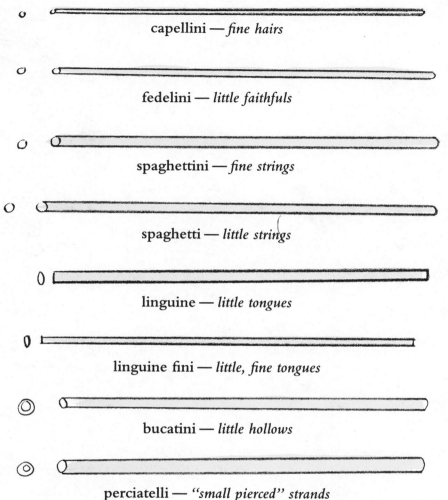

capellini — *fine hairs*

fedelini — *little faithfuls*

spaghettini — *fine strings*

spaghetti — *little strings*

linguine — *little tongues*

linguine fini — *little, fine tongues*

bucatini — *little hollows*

perciatelli — *"small pierced" strands*

Long Strands — the thinner strands for simple, olive oil–based sauces, seafood sauces, herb sauces such as pesto, and butter or olive oil–based tomato sauces. The thicker strands for tangy tomato sauces, spicy sauces, and meat sauces

tubetti — *little tubes*

elbows

sedani — *celery stalks*

gnocchetti rigati —
thin rigatoni

rigatoni — *big ridges*

sedanini —
little celery stalks

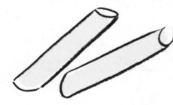

penne — *quills*

penne piccoline —
little quills

penne rigate —
ridged quills

Tubular Shapes — the smaller shapes for light tomato sauces, sauces with ricotta, butter sauces with small vegetable pieces; the larger shapes for olive oil–based sauces, thick meat ragùs, sauces with ricotta, sauces with large chunks of vegetables, tangy sauces, and in baked pasta dishes

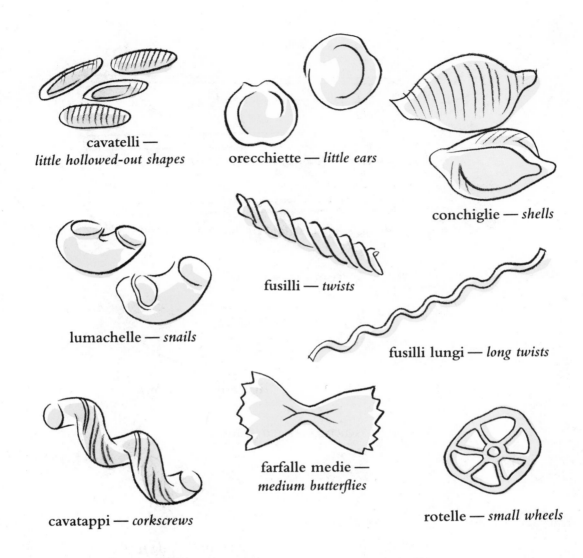

cavatelli — *little hollowed-out shapes*

orecchiette — *little ears*

conchiglie — *shells*

lumachelle — *snails*

fusilli — *twists*

fusilli lungi — *long twists*

cavatappi — *corkscrews*

farfalle medie — *medium butterflies*

rotelle — *small wheels*

Assorted Other Shapes — with olive oil–based sauces, tomato sauces, light meat sauces, sauces with small bits of vegetables, sauces with mozzarella; the largest available conchiglie and lumachelle for stuffing and baking

LONG STRANDS:

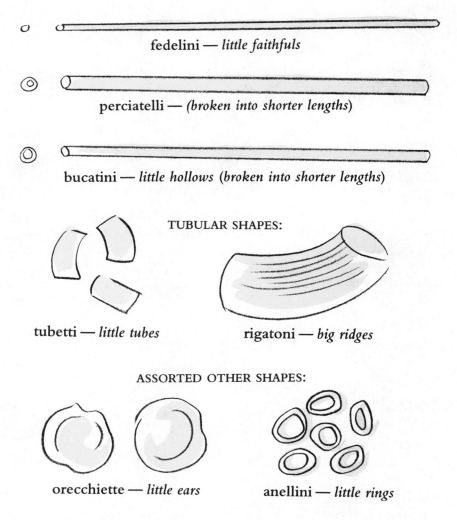

fedelini — *little faithfuls*

perciatelli — *(broken into shorter lengths)*

bucatini — *little hollows (broken into shorter lengths)*

TUBULAR SHAPES:

tubetti — *little tubes*

rigatoni — *big ridges*

ASSORTED OTHER SHAPES:

orecchiette — *little ears*

anellini — *little rings*

For Baked Pasta — with meat sauces, tomato sauces combined with cheeses such as ricotta and mozzarella, with salame, layered with vegetables, stuffed in vegetables

LA GUIDA

Fresh Egg Pasta

Fresh egg pasta dough, or *pasta all'uovo,* consists of creamy white unbleached all-purpose or semolina flour and fertile eggs. It is used with delicate sauces that do not mask the flavors of the dough: cream sauces, butter sauces, sweet vegetables, such as peas or asparagus, rich cheeses, such as mascarpone, and highly aromatic ingredients, like truffles or wild mushrooms cooked in butter. It is always used in making stuffed pasta and lasagna. When made with all-purpose flour, fresh pasta will not have the al dente quality of dried pasta, but instead will be meltingly tender to the bite. It should not be rubbery or gummy-tasting.

Buying fresh pasta is a perfectly respectable thing to do. Italians frequently buy it from the local bakery or pasta shop. Nowadays, few people other than grandmothers have the time to make pasta at home on a regular basis. Buying fresh pasta in America is tricky. Usually the dough is extruded rather than rolled, and when poorly made it has a slick, nonporous surface, which results in a rubbery, slippery pasta that doesn't absorb sauce. Most companies feel that for fresh pasta to be really fresh it should still be damp. What you often end up with is a clump of damp fettucine, usually horribly stuck together. This pasta has no chance of cooking evenly or of producing a good texture when cooked. Fresh pasta must dry out sufficiently before it is cooked. In fact, even when it is completely dried, *pasta all'uovo,* egg pasta, is considered to be the same product as fresh. However, finding a source for high-quality fresh pasta here is not easy. If you are desperate, buy imported dried egg pasta rather than the inferior fresh American deli-type pasta described above.

Fresh Egg Pasta Shapes

quadrucci — *little squares*

tagliarini — *fine cut*

Small, Short Shapes for Soup — in clear beef broth, chicken broth, and light soups

Long, Thin Strands for Soup — in clear broths and light vegetable soups

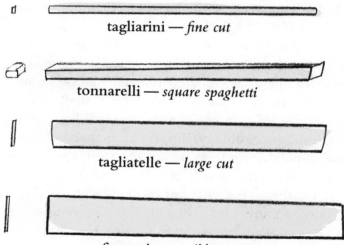

tagliarini — *fine cut*

tonnarelli — *square spaghetti*

tagliatelle — *large cut*

fettuccine — *ribbons*

Long Strands — for butter and cream sauces, butter-based vegetable sauces, meat sauces, herb sauces such as pesto, and tomato sauces

ravioli

mezzaluna — *half moon*

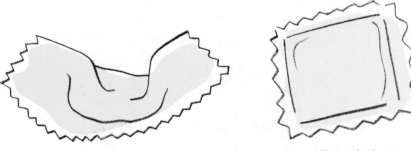

casonsei

tortelli — *little pies*

Stuffed Pasta — with butter and herb sauces, fresh tomato sauces, cream sauces; for stuffing, with ricotta, sweet vegetables, and mild herbs

fettuccine — *ribbons*

lasagna

Pasta al Forno — layered and baked with tomato sauces, meat sauces, béchamel

If a shape called for in a recipe is not available, use one that is its approximate size and shape from the same category; that is, if we call for sedanini in a recipe, and it is difficult to locate, substitute penne rigate.

Making Fresh Egg Dough
for Pasta

Making fresh egg pasta is one of those activities best learned at the side of someone who has done it over and over again for years. If you are highly motivated to learn to make good fresh egg pasta, we strongly recommend that you take a class in a local cooking school. When you watch experienced hands turn the flour and eggs expertly into yellow strands of fragrant pasta, you learn the texture of the dough, what kind of pressure to apply to the rolling pin (if the pasta is made by hand), or how to use the rollers (if it is made by machine). It is a simple, organically learned process because the expertise is handed down from experienced cook to novice. There are some things better learned in person; fresh pasta making is one of them.

The character of the dough will be determined by the flour and eggs you choose. We give you two standard recipes for egg pasta. Pasta all'Uovo I is the true traditional pasta. Made in the Emilia-Romagna style traditional in Bologna where fresh pasta is king *and* queen, this dough uses only all-purpose unbleached flour and eggs — no salt and no oil. This type of dough is good for meltingly tender fettuccine and for stuffed pasta where the softness of a dough made only with all-purpose flour is needed for pliability.

Pasta all'Uovo II uses a mixture of all-purpose flour and semolina, a hard-wheat or durum flour. If you wish, you may use only semolina flour in this recipe. Most restaurants that make their own pasta with large machines use a semolina-based dough. Because the dough is made with hard-wheat flour, it has a stiffer texture than that made with all-purpose flour. We do not recommend attempting to hand-roll dough made with semolina, but a hand-cranked machine works very well with it. We do not like the new extrusion machine made for home use. The dies used to extrude the dough into different shapes are made of plastic and produce a slick pasta that does not absorb sauce well. Of the two dough recipes, we tend to use the semolina recipe more often because we like the firm bite the durum flour adds to the pasta. Semolina comes packaged in different grinds. For pasta it is important to use the finest-ground semolina. It is as powdery as all-purpose flour and should feel soft between your fingertips.

In Italy many home cooks still have access to freshly laid farm eggs. The incredible bright orange yolks add flavor and nourishment to the pasta as well as tinting the dough a rich deep yellow. We recommend seeking out a source for fresh fertile eggs. They are more healthful and the yolks usually have more color than pale grocery eggs.

Proportions for Making Pasta all'Uovo

It is difficult to give exact proportions in recipes for fresh pasta, as even with these simple ingredients variabilities in weather and egg size can make a difference. The recipes below are meant as a guide. Add more or less flour as you need it to make a firm yet pliable dough. If you can find huge jumbo eggs, try using a proportion of 1 cup flour to 1 egg. After a while, making pasta will become such a comfortable activity that you will instinctively be aware of the variables involved in determining the proportion of flour and egg. The recipes below produce approximately 1¼ pounds of pasta suitable for 4 to 6 servings.

Pasta all'Uovo I

A light tender dough, perfect for stuffed pastas or fettuccine. Make dough following directions either for the Hand Method or Food Processor Method (see page 35).

2 *cups all-purpose unbleached flour*	3 *extra-large eggs*

Pasta all'Uovo II

A sturdy dough which cooks nicely al dente. Our favorite for most long, fresh pasta shapes. Try using all-semolina flour. Use the Food Processor Method (see page 35) for mixing the dough.

1 *cup all-purpose unbleached flour*	3 *extra-large eggs, beaten*
1 *cup semolina or hard durum-wheat flour*	

Pasta Integrale

(Fresh Whole-Wheat Pasta)

Whole-wheat pasta is a rich light brown color and has a subtle nutty flavor. It is not as strongly flavored as you might imagine. We pair it most often with slightly bitter greens or vegetables like rapini, Belgian endive, and radicchio. Make this dough using the Food Processor Method (see page 35).

1½ *cups all-purpose unbleached flour*	2 *teaspoons extra-virgin olive oil*
1½ *cups whole-wheat flour*	4 *extra-large eggs, beaten*
Pinch of salt	

Place the flours and salt together in the processor bowl. Pulse 2 or 3 times to mix the dry ingredients together. Continue, following the directions given for the Food Processor Method (see page 35), adding the extra-virgin olive oil at the same time that you add the eggs.

Pasta Verde

The bright green color of the dough results from using uncooked spinach. We use spinach dough mainly for simple baked lasagne. Make this dough using the Food Processor Method (see page 35) and by following additional instructions below.

2 *pounds fresh spinach, stems removed*

3 *cups all-purpose unbleached flour*

4 *extra-large eggs, beaten*

Wash the spinach well in several changes of water. Drain and dry the spinach and place it in a food processor with a steel blade, and pulse until the spinach is coarsely chopped. Add flour and process until spinach and flour are well mixed. Continue according to the instructions for the Food Processor Method (see page 35).

Pasta allo Zafferano

A dough with incredible color and rich flavor, we enjoy pairing it with simple ingredients, or using it to great effect for a stuffed pasta. To make dough following the Hand Method instructions (see page 35), add the saffron and water to the eggs. If using the Food Processor Method (see page 35) add the saffron and water (see instructions below) before you add the eggs.

¼ *ounce saffron threads*

¼ *cup water*

2 *cups all-purpose unbleached flour*

3 *extra-large eggs, beaten*

Boil the saffron threads in the water for 2 minutes. Let stand at least ½ hour before continuing with the recipe.

Pasta all'Erbe

Perhaps the simplest and most effective of the special pasta doughs. Using the Food Processor Method (see below), it is easy to add fresh basil, thyme, or Italian parsley to Pasta all'Uovo I or Pasta all'Uovo II. Simply add approximately 1 large bunch of cleaned, dried, roughly chopped herbs to the beaten egg and continue following directions.

Food Processor Method
for Mixing Dough

The doughs for Pasta all'Uovo I, Pasta all'Uovo II, and Pasta Integrale are easily made in a food processor. For Pasta all'Uovo II, put all the flour in the bowl with the steel blade. Beat the eggs together separately before adding them to the flour. Do not add all the eggs at once for, depending on the humidity, you may need less than is called for in the recipe. Pulse the machine until the eggs and flour come together in a mixture that resembles coffee bean–sized pellets. Turn the rough mixture out onto a board and firmly knead it together into a stiff dough. Continue using the directions for machine-rolled dough (see page 37). Before you roll the dough into pasta sheets, allow it to rest, covered with a kitchen towel, for at least 15 minutes.

Hand Method for Mixing Dough

Make a mound of flour on a wooden or marble board. Using your fingers, hollow a wide hole out of the center of the mound so that the flour looks like the crater of a volcano. Carefully break each egg separately into a cup to make sure it is fresh and good, then transfer it to the crater. Using a dinner fork with long tines, carefully beat the eggs until they are well scrambled. Keep beating the eggs and begin to slowly incorporate flour from the sides of the crater. Take care that the loose egg and flour batter in the center is kept enclosed on all sides by the mound of flour. When the egg mixture is very thick, and you can no longer mix in any more flour by beating with the fork, carefully push the remaining flour over the mixture and begin to knead it with your hands. Knead the mixture for several minutes until it absorbs as much flour as possible. After approximately 10 minutes of kneading, you should have a stiff but elastic dough. The beauty of this method is that if you have an excess of flour for the amount of egg, the extra flour will automatically fall away to the side and will not become incorporated into the dough. Before you roll the dough into pasta sheets, allow it to rest, covered with a kitchen towel, for at least 15 minutes.

To Roll Pasta by Hand

To roll pasta by hand you will need a straight, narrow rolling pin that does not have tapered ends. While rolling dough by hand, it is good to remember that hand-rolled pasta is a stretched dough rather than a compressed dough, which is the result of machine rolling. Keeping this in mind, take care to use a light, easy rolling motion with the rolling pin. You want to stretch the dough, not press it in onto itself. Also keep in mind that speed is an important element in making fresh pasta. As you feel more comfortable with the process, try to roll the dough out as quickly as possible to prevent it from becoming too leathery to roll properly.

Take the kneaded pasta dough and place it in the center of a large wooden or marble board. Using the rolling pin, lightly beat the dough 2 or 3 times so that it flattens a bit. Begin to roll out the dough by placing the rolling pin always one third up the pasta circle and gently rolling outward. Each time you roll up and out, move the pasta circle a quarter-turn to the right. Every time you make four quarter-turns, flip the circle of dough over and continue rolling outward. In this way you will stretch the cells of the dough equally in all directions.

When the dough is approximately $1/16$ inch thick, you can begin the process that really stretches the dough. Place the rolling pin at the top of the circle of dough and while lightly rolling toward you, curl one quarter of the pasta onto the rolling pin. Gently curve your hands over the rolling pin and slide them from side to side while simultaneously rolling the pin back and forth. Unroll the pasta circle, rotate it a quarter-turn, and repeat the curling of the dough around the rolling pin and the hand-stretching/ pin-rolling movement. This movement stretches the dough simultaneously in both directions and results in the extremely porous quality of handmade dough. Continue repeating this process until the sheet of dough is so thin you can see the pattern of your work surface through it.

If the pasta sheet, or *sfoglia*, is to be used for stuffed pasta, use it immediately. For fettuccine or other noodle shapes, it is necessary to allow *sfoglia* to dry just enough so that it won't stick to itself during the cutting process. Lay the sheet of dough on a lightly floured bedsheet or a few tea towels. Turn it occasionally. It should dry just enough to take on a leathery appearance, yet not so much that it becomes brittle. Drying will take between 15 to 30 minutes, depending on how warm and/or humid it is.

To cut noodles by hand, first roll the pasta sheet into a flat roll, 3 inches wide. Using a sharp knife, cut across the roll, creating whatever width you desire. When you have finished cutting the entire roll, gently toss the noodles to open them up and lay them on a clean, dry surface to dry for at least 5 minutes before cooking.

To Roll Pasta Using a Pasta Machine

Unwrap the ball of dough, which has rested for at least 15 minutes, and carefully cut a slice 1 inch thick and rewrap the remaining pasta. Flatten the pasta slice with the heel of your hand. If the dough feels a little tacky, lightly coat each side with flour. Open the pasta-machine rollers to their widest point. Begin to feed the pasta through the rollers. Repeat at this thickness 4 or 5 times, each time folding the sheet of pasta onto itself in thirds. Then roll the sheet of pasta, passing it through each successive number until you achieve the thickness you desire. For stuffed pastas, roll the dough as thin as the machine allows. For fettuccine, use the thinnest or second thinnest setting. For tonnarelli, use the third thinnest setting. When you roll the pasta for the last time, it will be easier to handle if you cut the sheet into 14-inch pieces as it comes out of the machine. Use flour only as necessary to prevent the pasta sheet from sticking to the rollers.

If you use the pasta sheet, *sfoglia,* for stuffed pasta, use it immediately. To use the *sfoglia* for fettuccine or other noodle shapes, it is necessary to allow the sheet to dry just enough so that it won't stick to itself during the cutting process. Lay the sheet of dough on a lightly floured bedsheet or a few tea towels. Turn it occasionally. It should dry just enough to take on a leathery appearance, yet not so much that it becomes brittle. Drying will take approximately 15 to 30 minutes depending on how warm and/or humid it is.

Cutting Pasta Sheets into Different Shapes

Tagliatelle — One must cut this traditional Emilia-Romagna shape by hand because the cutters on pasta machines produce a narrower cut. First, roll the thin pasta sheet into a flat roll 3 inches wide. Using a sharp knife, cut across the roll to create noodles that are slightly less than ¼ inch wide. When you have finished cutting the entire roll, gently toss the noodles to open them up, laying them on a clean, dry surface to dry for at least 5 minutes before cooking.

Quadrucci — Cut the pasta as you would for tagliatelle, then cut across the still-rolled noodles to create little squares.

Tagliarini — Roll the pasta sheets as thin as possible. Cut the pasta using the narrow cutting blades on your pasta machine.

Fettuccine — Roll the pasta sheets as thin as possible. Cut the pasta using the wider cutting blades on your pasta machine.

Tonnarelli — Roll the pasta sheets to a thickness similar to dried spaghetti. It should be the third thinnest setting on the pasta machine. Cut the pasta using the narrow cutting blades of your pasta machine.

Cooking and Serving Pasta

Fresh pasta and dried pasta are cooked in the same way. To cook 1 pound dried pasta or 1½ pounds fresh pasta, bring about 4 quarts of water to a boil in a large pot and add 1 heaping tablespoon of salt. Salting the water is an important step; without it the pasta tastes bland. To cook a larger quantity, increase the amount of water and salt proportionally. Use two pots if necessary. Do not try to cook too much pasta in too little water! There will not be enough room for the water to circulate around the pasta, which will cook unevenly and have a tendency to stick together. Do not add olive oil to the water and do not rinse the pasta after cooking it. This used to be done to prevent poor-quality American dried pasta from sticking together. With high-quality dried Italian pasta there is no need. There is just enough surface starch left on the pasta for the sauce to adhere to it but not enough for the pasta to stick to itself.

Add the pasta to the water all at once, and stir immediately with a wooden spoon to prevent it from sticking together. Put the lid back on the pot until the water returns to a boil. Remove the lid and stir again. Cook at a steady boil, stirring every so often to ensure that the pasta does not stick. Begin testing the pasta well before you think it is ready. Bite a strand or cut it to determine how cooked it is. Never time pasta. There are so many variables that the timing can never be accurate. The only true gauge is your own sense of when the pasta is ready, backed up by repeated testing. Fresh pasta takes very little time to become tender — just a brief cooking after the water returns to a boil. Dried pasta takes longer, and the timing varies greatly from one shape to another. When dried pasta is al dente, firm at the center but tender, drain into a sturdy stainless steel colander with handles. With fresh stuffed pasta, lift out of the water with a slotted spoon or Chinese strainer. Sometimes it is necessary to add a little pasta water to a sauce to achieve the right consistency. Check the sauce recipe before throwing away the pasta water.

The pasta is now ready to be sauced. Toss the sauce with the pasta very low in the serving bowl. Theatrically tossing the pasta high in the air only serves to cool it off. Often a lump of butter or a little olive oil is mixed with the pasta in the serving bowl before the sauce is added. This helps carry the sauce further, and enriches it with a final fresh flavor. Many people contend that the proper time to add cheese to pasta is before adding the sauce. In this way it melts instantly in contact with the hot pasta. When serving stuffed pasta, the sauce usually is placed underneath the pasta, which shows off the intricacies of the particular pasta shape, or the sauce is gently spooned on top. Tossing stuffed pastas would break them.

Serve all pastas in shallow soup bowls. Flat plates cause the pasta to cool off too quickly, and have no edge against which to brace your fork for twirling.

All of the above steps must be carried out quickly. The pasta must be drained the second you have determined it is ready. If not, it will overcook. It must be mixed with the sauce right away, or it may begin to stick to itself. And it must be served quickly to be really good. If all this urgency sounds stressful, it really isn't. After a few tries, you'll find it becomes a natural physical series of motions. Before you know it, the pasta is on the table. Remember to assemble everyone at the table first, before you sauce the pasta.

Cheese is not always served with pasta, although it is a frequent accompaniment. Seafood sauces are never served with cheese. Some sauces may taste a little sweeter or lighter without the addition of Parmesan or Pecorino Romano cheese. Taste the pasta first to see if you think it needs it. Do not just automatically blanket the pasta with cheese. It should be an accent, not the main taste. In southern Italy, dried toasted bread crumbs are used to top pasta with delicious results. Warm, nutty-tasting bread crumbs grace all kinds of pasta sauces, especially those with seafood in them. The bread crumbs absorb the juices of the sauce, and adhere to long strands of pasta, helping the sauce flavor all surfaces of the pasta.

La Dispensa

The Pantry

A well-stocked pantry will provide an almost limitless variety of pasta dishes at literally a moment's notice. Take a trip to the local Italian market to begin your adventure. The initial outlay will reward you with many delicious meals.

Start by selecting many different pasta shapes, from tiny stars to big, chunky pastas, and of course long strands of pasta from finest to thickest, round and flat. Choose a good extra-virgin olive oil, one that fits your budget so that you feel free to use it often. Find a good-quality red wine vinegar that is fragrant and mellow, and a bottle of rich, almost syrupy balsamic vinegar. Buy a varied assortment of packaged dried beans and canned cooked beans. Look for Italian canned beans that are made without preservatives or additives.

Down the condiment aisle find plump sun-dried tomatoes, rich, lustrous black olive paste, firm little capers, and cream-colored dried porcini mushroom caps. Select two or three cans each of anchovies, sardines, and tuna packed in olive oil. Down the next aisle are the all-important canned imported Italian tomatoes. Buy four or five differing brands, if possible, so you can experiment to determine which is your favorite. Also pick up a tube or two of tomato paste.

Your basket is filling up nicely now, but there is still room for the spices. Get a fresh bottle of dried oregano (throw out the old bottle at home). Also buy a fresh supply of crushed and whole red chiles and some fresh black peppercorns. If you do not already have one, invest in a high-quality, reliable pepper mill. Get some good sea salt, both fine and coarsely ground. Splurge on saffron — there is nothing else like it for adding that special exotic flavor and beautiful color. Go to the refrigerated cases and select some oil-cured black olives and plump green and black olives in brine. Ask to taste the olives first to be sure they have good texture and flavor. Buy chunks of Parmesan and Pecorino Romano cheeses. To round things out you need only a few bottles of wine.

A quick stop at the local market is next. Buy onions, garlic, fresh tomatoes, lemons, and some aromatic basil and parsley. By now, your hunger has probably reached peak. At home, store all your purchases, open a bottle of wine, take a few sips, and decide which pasta to prepare for dinner.

ANCHOVIES

Small cans of flat anchovies packed in olive oil are generally available. Consider stocking the 1-pound 12-ounce size if you use them frequently. Make sure the anchovies are kept covered with olive oil by topping off the container with oil as you use them. Keep refrigerated. The anchovies should be firm and look like small fillets, which is what they are. In Italy anchovies are also sold whole, packed in salt. Sometimes they are found in Italian markets here. To prepare the anchovies, scrape off the salt and fillet them. Pack fillets in a jar and cover with olive oil. Anchovies are often used in Italian cooking in place of salt because in addition to their renowned saltiness they add a depth of flavor to sauces. A few anchovies melted into a tomato sauce give the finished dish a deeper, richer flavor than just using salt alone.

BEANS

Cannellini beans, similar to Great Northern beans, are thin and white. Borlotti beans are mottled deep red and cream color and are shaped like a pinto bean. Garbanzo beans, or ceci, are golden yellow in color and almost spherical in shape. All beans except borlotti are usually available in bulk packages, or canned. Keep a variety on hand. Try to locate canned beans packed in Italy; they are free of additives and preservatives. Cannellini beans have a mild and creamy flavor. Borlotti beans, although not widely available in this country, are well worth the search. They have a rich, full flavor and an almost chalky texture that holds up well in soups and sauces. Garbanzo beans are nutty in taste. Pasta and beans are a time-honored tradition in Italian cooking. It is a deeply gratifying combination.

BREAD CRUMBS

Homemade from good plain bread that has no added flavoring. Break up into chunks bread that has completely dried out. Process chunks in a food processor with a steel blade or in a blender until crumbs are small but not reduced to a fine powder. Store in pantry in a jar with an airtight lid. They will last for months. They are often used toasted as a topping for pasta. To toast, place bread crumbs in a large skillet over medium heat. Stir constantly until golden. Immediately transfer to a plate to cool.

CAPERS

Capers are the unopened buds of a shrub that grows in the Mediterranean, and are cured in vinegar. Generally available, the small ones tend to have better flavor and texture than the larger ones. Taste a caper by itself to experience what it is all about. Rinse the capers first if you prefer to remove some of the excess vinegar. Capers add piquant accents to sauces and are often paired with olives.

CHEESES

Parmesan–Of all the ingredients most closely associated with Italian food, Parmesan cheese is one of the most used and beloved by Americans. Real Italian Parmesan is called Parmigiano-Reggiano, and is part of a family of cheeses called "Grana." The two primary cheeses in the Grana family are Grana Padano and Parmigiano-Reggiano. Both are cow's-milk cheeses that are aged for grating. Of the two, the Reggiano, as it is often called, is of higher quality. More rich, buttery, and sweet in flavor than the Grana Padano, Reggiano is also moister, which makes it a great cheese for eating in small chunks with antipasti or fruit. However, there is a substantial price difference between the two cheeses. So if price makes the difference between using an imported or a domestic cheese on your pasta, please use the Grana Padano. We feel that American Parmesan is not an option. If you want to splurge, buy a chunk of Reggiano just to taste the difference. A little goes a long way.

Store the Parmesan chunk in the refrigerator, tightly wrapped. Grate only the amount you need just before using it. Rewrap the chunk and return it to the refrigerator. Often Americans go overboard in their appreciation of Parmesan. It isn't necessary to drown the pasta with grated cheese, and in fact there are several sauces that do not require cheese at all. We give appropriate suggestions for cheese accompaniment in the recipes. Parmesan is used on milder sauces where a mellow, nutty cheese flavor is desired. In the recipes the word Parmesan refers to either Reggiano or Grana Padano.

Pecorino Romano–Pecorino Romano is a sheep's milk cheese which is aged for grating. As with Parmesan, buy it by the chunk and store it in the refrigerator, tightly wrapped. Grate only what you need for one meal and return the chunk to the refrigerator. Pecorino Romano has a sharp flavor that is more acidic and tangy than Parmesan. It is used to enliven simple vegetable sauces and with certain southern Italian pasta dishes. Because of the availability of sheep's milk in southern Italy, Pecorino Romano is often used more frequently than Parmesan.

HERBS, DRIED

Oregano–This is one herb we use more often dried than fresh. Most available Mediterranean oregano comes from Greece. Buy Greek oregano rather than Mexican oregano, which is more assertive in flavor and tends to be too harsh for Italian food. Try to overcome the pizza parlor associations that may come to mind. It is not the fault of oregano that it was strewn over a lot of bad Italian food. Use oregano sparingly to add a strong, almost bitter perfumed note to sauces made with fresh tomato, mozzarella, or as an accent to sweet scallops, etc.

HERBS, FRESH

Basil–Buy basil that is bright green and fragrant. Look for a source that carries the small-leaf variety; it has more fragrance and pungency. Pack loosely in a plastic bag, and store in the refrigerator until needed. Clean basil by gently wiping dirt off leaves with a damp paper towel. Basil wilts and blackens rapidly when wet. Chop right before using. The perfume of basil is one of the glories of the Italian kitchen, so try to find a source for the freshest, most pungent leaves.

Italian or Flat-leaf Parsley–Its large tender leaves and intense, bracing bouquet make this parsley superior to the curly-leaf variety most commonly found in markets. Curly parsley lacks a cleansing herbal aroma and it has tougher leaves than the flat-leaf variety. Italian parsley is becoming more widely available and is well worth the search. Store in a plastic bag in the refrigerator. After washing, dry very well. Chop right before using. We use parsley so frequently in cooking that we will clean and chop an entire bunch before preparing the meal. In this way it is easy to have handfuls ready to toss into the dish. An underappreciated herb. We use parsley as often as we do basil.

LEMONS

Look for thin-skinned lemons that feel juicy. Keep in a dry place. Refrigerate only if turning soft. The refreshing acidic, highly fragrant juice and zest add a special zip to sauces.

OLIVE OIL, EXTRA VIRGIN

To be labeled extra-virgin, olive oil must have no more than 1.5 percent acidity, and must be obtained from the first pressing of the olives. There is a vocabulary used in judging extra-virgin olive oil just as there is in judging wine. Each region produces an oil with certain characteristics. Its taste can be fruity, nutty, or peppery; it can be of light, medium, or heavy viscosity. Its color can range from lightly golden to a deep green. As with wines, the only way to make sense of the tremendous selection available is to begin by tasting a few at a time, until you have a sense of the range of flavors. Settle on a few types that you enjoy and that are in your price range. Availability may fluctuate, so be flexible.

To get started, select an Italian extra-virgin olive oil. To be sure, all Mediterranean countries produce good oil; in fact, much oil now packed in Italy originated in Spain or Greece. Unfortunately, we cannot recommend California olive oil, as it is extremely viscous and has an unpleasant heavy flavor. Extra-virgin oil should last for about six months if kept away from heat and out of direct sunlight. Do not refrigerate it—this alters the flavor. Buy oil in small quantities at first until you can gauge how quickly you go through a bottle or can. Extra-virgin olive oil is the single most important factor in Italian cooking. It creates the flavor base. If we were banished to a desert island and could have only one luxury, we would opt for an inexhaustible supply of good extra-virgin oil.

OLIVE OIL, PURE

A lesser grade of oil, used primarily for frying.

OLIVES

In Brine–Select imported black and green olives in brine, found either in bulk in the refrigerated case of an Italian market or in jars from importers of high-quality Mediterranean products. The olives should be crisp and have a clean, tangy flavor. When buying olives in bulk, ask to taste one first. Unpitted olives have the best texture and flavor. Olives in brine add piquant meatiness to sauces. Because green olives are the unripe fruit of the tree, they have a sharper flavor. Use them when you really want to add zip to a sauce. Two varieties of black olives we use often are Kalamata (Greek) and Gaeta (Italian).

Oil-Cured Black Olives–Glossy black with a lightly wrinkled surface, oil-cured olives are most easily found in Italian or Middle Eastern delis. These olives should have a meaty texture and hold their shape during cooking. Avoid any that are too dry or excessively salty. Good black olives are the heart and soul of Mediterranean cooking. They should have a bouquet that is almost like wine—dark, rich, and pungent. They add depth of flavor to sauces.

Olive Paste–Available packed in small jars, this product is a *pesto,* or paste, of black olives and olive oil, sometimes with herbs added. It is a rich, smooth paste that embodies the tangy essence of olives. Use it in small quantities in combination with less assertive ingredients. We pair it with cream and mild cheeses. It may also be spread on good country bread.

ONIONS AND GARLIC

Look for firm onions and garlic bulbs that have not sprouted. Store in a dry, dark place.

PASTA, DRIED (MANY SHAPES AND SIZES)

Buy a variety of imported Italian pasta shapes for soups, sauced pastas, and baked pastas; get some imported whole-wheat pasta, some shapes for stuffing, and so forth. The selection seems almost endless. Be adventurous and try different shapes. Each shape reacts differently to a sauce, and has a different look on the plate. The best way to really understand a pasta shape is to eat it.

PEPPER, BLACK

Whole peppercorns are available in any supermarket. Invest in a dependable, good-quality pepper mill. It will last for years and turn out to be an inexpensive investment. Grind fresh pepper directly onto the dish you are preparing. It is especially pleasing to grind some right before serving so that the fresh aroma of pepper wafts up with the steam of the hot dish. Black pepper is especially good in mild-flavored sauces, such as those made with ricotta or cream, where the fragrance and bite of the pepper stand out.

PEPPER, RED CHILE (WHOLE AND CRUSHED)

Red chile pepper is essential in making a number of pasta sauces. When red chile pepper is included in a recipe, black pepper is usually eliminated. The heat of the chiles helps a simple sauce stand up to the task of flavoring a big dish of pasta. Try to find whole cayenne peppers. Crush your own or buy red chile pepper flakes in jars.

PORCINI MUSHROOMS, DRIED

These intensely flavored dried mushrooms are available in small packages or in bulk. Look for large pieces of creamy caps. Dried porcini keep for months. They need to be soaked for about 20 minutes in warm water to cover before using. Dried porcini add a deep, strong, woodsy taste to sauces.

SAFFRON

Saffron is the deep orange, fragrant stigmas of the purple crocus. The tiny rusty-gold threads are still picked by hand today, hence their high price. Saffron is generally available in 1-ounce packets in the spice section of the supermarket and in good Italian delis. Just a pinch is needed to imbue a dish with dazzling color and unique flavor. Saffron is an ingredient of the classic northern Italian dish risotto alla Milanese, but it is also used in the Abruzzi, Sicily, and Sardinia. We use saffron to tint pasta by adding it to the dough or directly to the water used for boiling the pasta. There are a few special sauces where it imparts a characteristic flavor.

SARDINES

Whole sardines packed in olive oil are generally available in most super-markets. They are good to use in fast sauces when you want that taste of the sea.

SEA SALT, FINE AND COARSE-GROUND

A must for your pantry. Salt is essential to life. Depriving yourself of salt, unless instructed to do so by a doctor, is dangerous to your health. The primary threat to the American diet is in the quantities of heavily salted and preserved processed foods that are consumed by millions each year. Those of us who eat fresh, unprocessed foods can generally include salt as a normal part of a balanced diet. It is important to understand the function of salt in relationship to the flavor of food. It should not mask flavor, but instead be used to coax out the true taste of the food you are eating. For most people, when salt is used moderately, no harm results, only pleasure. Since pasta has a mild, bland taste that acts as a foil for sauces, it is imperative to salt the water in which it is cooked, or the dish will taste flat.

TOMATOES, CANNED IMPORTED

Look for plum-shaped tomatoes grown and packed in Italy. Called the San Marzano variety, they break down quickly to form a sauce. These tomatoes are packed in their own juices, sometimes with the addition of a basil leaf. They do not contain additives to firm or preserve them, and also sharpen and further acidify the flavor. Italian tomatoes are much easier to find now in Italian markets, specialty stores, and some supermarkets. You will find their sweet yet tart flavor makes a big difference when you prepare many of the tomato-based sauces in this book.

TOMATOES, FRESH

We recommend Roma tomatoes for sauce making. These small, plum-shaped tomatoes seem to have a better flavor and color than the round varieties most commonly found in supermarkets. Maybe the fact that they are not sought after by fast-food chains means that they are still bred for flavor instead of shipability. If you grow your own, or if you find other varieties of vine-ripened tomatoes that are deep red, firm, and heavy, by all means use those. Do not refrigerate tomatoes. The cold destroys their texture and stops the ripening process. When chopping tomatoes for raw sauces, we generally leave the skin on.

TOMATOES, SUN-DRIED

Available either packed in jars in olive oil or packed dry in plastic bags. Avoid any that are leathery or have a harsh, sweet flavor. The ones packed in plastic bags are usually too dry to revive successfully and are often full of seeds. Try drying your own during tomato season. (See our book *Cucina Fresca* for a recipe for Sun-Dried Tomatoes [page 276]). Remember that the tomatoes should remain a little moist. They can be used in a variety of ways: made into a paste for pasta sauces, cut into strips and added to other ingredients as a bright flavor note, or served as an antipasto.

TOMATO PASTE

Generally available in small cans or tubes in supermarkets and stores. This scarlet paste was originally made by drying cooked tomato sauce in the sun in large dishes until evaporation produced a concentrated paste. A small can of tomato paste goes a long way, but you can top off what remains in the can with a little olive oil to prevent darkening and spoilage. The convenience of the tomato-paste tube solves that problem. The paste is used when just a touch of tomato flavor is needed, but not the bulk of the pulp and juices or the cooking time involved.

TUNA, CANNED

Buy Italian-style tuna packed in olive oil. It is rich-tasting and tender. If difficult to find, buy chunk light or albacore tuna, whichever you prefer, packed in water or oil, and drain before using. Excellent for preparing fast sauces with a satisfying hearty element.

WINE, RED AND WHITE

Have several bottles of good red and white wines on hand. It goes without saying that wine is the ideal accompaniment to pasta.

Pasta a Minestra

Pasta Soups

*I*magine all the soul-satisfying qualities of soup and of pasta in one bowl!

We have included two examples of pasta served in clear chicken and beef broth. These soups are elegant, light first courses. We have also included soups that are more filling and contain an assortment of vegetables, enriched with egg, pesto, or cheese. They are appropriately served as the first course in a traditional Italian menu, or as the main part of a light meal.

Finally there are robust soups made of filling combinations of pasta with beans or with potatoes. These soups are examples of *la cucina povera,* peasant cooking. They are made of simple ingredients, generally without any broth, which can be assembled quickly with what is at hand. Usually these ingredients are household staples — dried beans, potatoes, pasta, onions — available all year round in the pantry. Even though the cooking time may be long for some of the recipes, the soups require very little attention. They are warming, main-dish soups for cold nights and hungry people.

Brodo di Pollo

CHICKEN BROTH

MAKES APPROXIMATELY 1 ½ QUARTS

This is the basic chicken broth used in Italian cooking. It is light yet rich in flavor, and requires a much shorter cooking time than classic French chicken stock because the flavor you want is less concentrated. The direct, fresh tastes of Italian cooking don't require the long cooking periods essential for more complex stocks. Organically raised free-range chickens produce a good rich broth. Don't forget to add chicken feet for a depth of flavor and richness. Always have some chicken broth on hand in the freezer for use in soups and risotti.

1 *2–3 pound whole chicken, with feet if possible*
1 *pound chicken backs and necks*
Water
1 *carrot, trimmed*
3 *stalks celery, trimmed*

3 *sprigs parsley*
2 *cloves garlic, peeled*
1 *bay leaf*
Salt to taste
Freshly ground black pepper to taste or a few peppercorns

Wash the chicken carefully, rinsing out any blood that remains in the cavity, and gently pull off the extra fat attached to the breast and tail areas. Place the whole chicken and the backs and necks in a soup pot. Cover with water so that it is 4 inches above the chicken and bones. Bring to a boil, and carefully skim off all the scum as it rises to the surface. When there is no more scum, add all the remaining ingredients, lower the heat, and simmer, partly covered, for at least 1 hour, or 2 hours for a richer broth. The more slowly the broth bubbles, the clearer the soup will be. Strain the broth, reserving the chicken and vegetables or discard them, if desired. Either use the broth immediately or refrigerate it for later use. If you do refrigerate it, remove the fat from the top when it has congealed.

Brodo di Pollo con Quadrucci

CHICKEN BROTH WITH EGG PASTA SQUARES

SERVES 4 TO 6

The eggy taste of the fresh pasta fills this broth with goodness. At the Ristorante Roma in Amatrice the bowl came to the table filled with the little squares, bathed in just enough broth to keep them floating. The great fun in eating this simple dish was enhanced by the biggest soup spoon we've ever seen.

1½ *cups leftover fresh pasta, cut into ¼-inch squares*	1 *teaspoon extra-virgin olive oil*
1½ *quarts Chicken Broth (see page 59)*	*Freshly grated Parmesan cheese*

Bring a pot of salted water to the boil. Add the quadrucci and blanch in boiling water for 1 minute, just to remove any excess starch. Quickly drain and gently run cold water over the pasta to stop the cooking process. Add 1 teaspoon of extra-virgin olive oil to the pasta to keep it from sticking together while you heat the broth. Bring the chicken broth to a boil. Add the quadrucci and gently cook a few minutes until the pasta squares are al dente. Serve immediately with grated Parmesan cheese on the side.

Brodo di Carne

BEEF BROTH

MAKES APPROXIMATELY 1½ QUARTS

*I*talian beef broth is light and flavorful. It is used for some soups, for most risotti, and as a moistening agent for braised meats. Don't confuse it with French beef stock, which is very strong, deep-flavored, and forms the basis for French cooking.

1 *pound boiling beef, such as flanken*
1 *pound beef bones, preferably marrow bones*
Water

1 *onion, unpeeled*
1 *carrot*
1 *stalk celery*
2 *small tomatoes*
1 *garlic clove, unpeeled*

Place the meat and the bones in a heavy soup pot. Cover with water and bring to a boil. Carefully skim away the scum as it rises to the top. When the broth is clear, add the remaining ingredients and turn down the heat so that the water barely simmers. Cook over low heat for approximately 3 hours. Strain the broth of bones and vegetables and discard. If using the broth for a clear soup, strain it again through 4 layers of cheesecloth. Refrigerate and remove fat when it has congealed.

Beef Broth with Anellini

Start with the most flavorful clear beef broth you can make (see page 61) and add the anellini. Any small pasta shape can be substituted, but we especially love the way the beautiful little rings of pasta look floating in the broth. We rinse the pasta first in cold water to avoid spoiling the beautiful clear broth with the pasta starch.

½ cup imported anellini or other very small pasta shape suitable for soup

1 teaspoon extra-virgin olive oil

1½ quarts flavorful clear beef broth

Freshly grated Parmesan cheese

Bring a pot of salted water to the boil. Add the anellini, turn down the heat, and simmer until they are almost done but slightly raw inside. Quickly drain and gently run cold water over the pasta to stop the cooking process. Add 1 teaspoon of extra-virgin olive oil to the pasta to keep it from sticking together. Bring the beef broth to a boil. Add the precooked anellini and gently simmer a few minutes until the rings of pasta are al dente. Serve immediately with grated Parmesan cheese on the side.

Pasta e Patate
PASTA AND POTATOES

*P*asta e Patate is a southern Italian dish often served in place of the pasta course. The traditional recipe adds more dried pasta than our recipe calls for, so the *minestra* (soup) becomes *asciutta* (dry), and is less a soup than a "wet" pasta. The potatoes that are added first should be completely soft at the end of the cooking time so that the starch thickens the soup. This is a good example of how to combine simple ingredients to produce a delicious and satisfying dish. Potatoes create a creamy texture that merges with the flavors of rosemary and tomato. If pancetta is unavailable, substitute lean salt pork or bacon blanched in boiling water to remove the smoked flavor.

¼ cup extra-virgin olive oil

1 onion, peeled and coarsely chopped

2 thin slices pancetta, coarsely chopped

2 stalks celery, washed and thinly sliced

2 large carrots, peeled and cut into large dice

2 small tomatoes, peeled, seeded, and coarsely chopped

1½ quarts water

3 potatoes, peeled and cut into 1-inch dice, divided

Freshly ground black pepper to taste

1 sprig fresh rosemary

½–1 cup imported elbow macaroni

Salt to taste

Heat the extra-virgin olive oil in a heavy-bottomed soup pot. Add the onion and pancetta. Cook over medium heat for a few minutes or until the onion just begins to soften. Add the celery, carrots, and tomatoes, stir to coat with the oil, and gently sauté for 5 minutes. Add the water, half the diced potatoes, pepper, and the rosemary. Bring the soup to a boil. Turn the heat down so that the mixture simmers and cook for approximately 45 minutes, stirring occasionally. The potatoes should be very soft. Add the rest of the potatoes, the dried pasta, and salt, and cook until the potatoes and the pasta are tender, adding a bit more water if necessary. The soup should be on the thick side, yet still be pourable.

Pasta e Lenticchie
PASTA AND LENTILS

SERVES 6 TO 8

*L*ike Pasta e Patate (see page 63), this soup is often made *asciutta*. Lentils, with their dark, earthy look and rich, almost spicy aroma produce a very flavorful soup without chicken or beef broth. An added bonus is the short cooking time. Our friends, the Sarnos, encourage the extravagant use of parsley. Its bracing green flavor enlivens the dusty taste of the lentils.

¼ *cup extra-virgin olive oil*

2 *thin slices pancetta, coarsely chopped*

1 *onion, peeled and coarsely chopped*

2 *celery stalks, thinly sliced*

3 *small tomatoes, peeled, seeded, and coarsely chopped*

1½ *quarts water*

¾ *cup lentils*

Freshly ground black pepper to taste

2 *large handfuls chopped Italian parsley*

½–1 *cup imported tubetti*

Salt

Heat the extra-virgin olive oil in a heavy soup pot. Add the pancetta and onion and cook over medium heat until the onion begins to soften. Add the celery and tomatoes. Stir well and continue to cook for approximately 5 minutes. Add the water, lentils, pepper, and parsley. Bring to a boil and cook until the lentils are tender and the soup is thick, adding water if necessary. Approximately 15 minutes before serving add the pasta and salt to taste. Cook at a low simmer, stirring frequently, until pasta is tender.

Pasta e Fagioli

WHITE BEAN SOUP WITH PASTA

*I*talians love the delicate taste of cannellini beans and use them often in soups, as a side dish, or pureed as a topping for bruschetta. They have a creamy texture and mild flavor that are perfectly suited to carry the flavors of fresh herbs and fine olive oil. Every Italian cook has a favorite way of preparing Pasta e Fagioli. From Rome southward, celery and/or carrots are the most commonly used vegetables. A Milanese friend contends that our version of white bean soup is *alla Toscana* because of the addition of the soffritto of basil, parsley, and garlic. This soup is best prepared *asciutta* (dry). The slow, gentle cooking helps to keep the beans intact.

1 *pound cannellini or large white beans*	10 *large fresh basil leaves, chopped*
Water	*Salt and freshly ground black pepper to taste*
1 *small onion, peeled and coarsely chopped*	½–1 *cup imported spaghetti, broken into small, irregular pieces*
½ *cup extra-virgin olive oil, divided*	1 *large tomato, peeled, seeded, and coarsely chopped (optional)*
2–3 *garlic cloves, peeled and minced*	
Handful chopped Italian parsley	

Pick through the beans and discard any discolored or broken ones and any stones. Rinse beans gently but thoroughly under cold running water. Place them in a large bowl with enough water to cover by several inches. Let them soak overnight or for at least 6 hours. When ready to cook the beans, place them with their liquid and the coarsely chopped onion in a heavy-bottomed soup pot. Add enough water to cover beans by 3 inches. Heat slowly to just below boiling. The beans should not move very much in the water. Keep the water at a point where it barely simmers. Cook for 2 to 3 hours or until beans are nearly cooked. They should be tender yet hold their shape.

Place half the extra-virgin olive oil in a small skillet and heat over a moderate flame. Add the garlic, parsley, and basil. Sauté briefly, just until the herbs give off an aroma. Add the sautéed herbs and the extra-virgin olive oil to the beans. Add the remaining oil and salt and pepper. Add tomato, if desired. Continue cooking the beans until they are completely tender. Before serving add the pasta and, stirring often, cook until pasta is al dente and soup has thickened. Serve immediately. Pass a cruet of extra-virgin olive oil to top the soup.

Spaghetti and Broccoli Soup

SERVES 4 TO 6

What could be easier to assemble than a soup of spaghetti and broccoli? Because of the general availability of the ingredients, you can put together this soup at a moment's notice. Serve it often. It's flavorful, fresh tasting, and healthful.

2 *pounds tender, fresh broccoli*
1½ *quarts water*
Salt
1–2 *cups imported spaghetti,*
    broken into 1-inch lengths

¼ *cup extra-virgin olive oil*
Freshly grated Pecorino
    Romano cheese (optional)

Use only very young, green broccoli and peel the stalks. Trim bottoms of stalks and discard any old or tough sections. Cut stalks and flowerets into bite-sized pieces. Put the water into a large pot and bring to a boil. Add salt, stir, then add the broccoli. Cover and cook over medium heat for about 5 minutes. Add the broken spaghetti, stir, and cook until the pasta is al dente. Taste for salt. It will probably require more. Before serving, turn off heat and stir in the extra-virgin olive oil. Cover and let rest for a few minutes. Serve with Pecorino Romano cheese, if desired.

Stracciatella Reale
FANCY EGG DROP SOUP

SERVES 4 TO 6

*M*arco Polo meets Columbus in this soup. Elegant and sweet-tasting with the added nourishment of egg. Stracciatella means "little rags," which is how the threads of egg look in the soup. Marjoram gives it an intensely floral bouquet. Of all the herbs it is the one most difficult to place. Marjoram is most often teamed with mild foods that have a touch of sweetness to them. Even though marjoram is not used as often as other herbs, it's a delight to grow in the garden. Its perfume fills the air, and it produces a profusion of little white flowers that attract bees from miles around.

¼ *cup extra-virgin olive oil*
1 *garlic clove, peeled and minced*
1 *large zucchini, ends trimmed, diced*
1½ *quarts chicken broth*
2 *tomatoes, peeled, seeded, and cut lengthwise into thin strips*
1 *10-ounce package frozen peas*

1 *sprig fresh marjoram, chopped*
¼ *pound imported capellini or*
½ *pound fresh tagliarini*
Salt and freshly ground black pepper to taste
½ *cup freshly grated Parmesan cheese*
2 *eggs, lightly beaten*

Heat the extra-virgin olive oil in a soup pot. Add the garlic and cook until it gives off its characteristic aroma. Add the diced zucchini and sauté over low heat for 1 to 2 minutes. Add the chicken broth, tomatoes, peas, and fresh marjoram. Cook over medium heat just until the peas and zucchini are tender. The soup may be prepared ahead up to this point. About 10 minutes before serving bring the soup to a boil and add the pasta. Stir and cook until pasta is al dente, adding salt and pepper. Meanwhile, in a bowl beat together the Parmesan cheese and the eggs. Just before serving turn down the heat so that the soup barely simmers. Add the beaten egg mixture all at once while stirring. As soon as the eggs cook, serve immediately.

Minestra di Pasta e Fave
FAVA BEAN SOUP WITH PASTA

SERVES 4 TO 6

*L*ike many of our soups, this one does not require a broth. Water is the cooking medium. It is easy to assemble; the time-consuming task is shelling the favas. It is imperative to remove the thin, waxy outer layer of each individual bean for the favas to become tender and soft. Shelling beans is an activity best combined with leisurely conversation. These tasks should not be viewed as burdensome but rather as welcome, calm, unhurried moments.

2 pounds fresh, tender fava beans, unshelled weight

3 tablespoons extra-virgin olive oil

2 slices pancetta, chopped

1 small onion, peeled and finely diced

¼ cup chopped Italian parsley

1 celery stalk, strings removed, finely diced

½ cup imported canned Italian tomatoes, chopped

Salt and freshly ground black pepper to taste

1½ quarts water

1½ cups imported dried cavatelli

¼ cup grated Pecorino Romano cheese, plus additional for table use

Shell the fava beans and gently peel off the skin of each bean. Set beans aside. In a large soup pot combine the extra-virgin olive oil, pancetta, onion, parsley, and celery. Sauté over low heat until vegetables soften. Add the tomatoes, season with salt and pepper, and simmer for 10 minutes. Add the fava beans and toss with the tomato mixture for a few minutes. Add water and bring to a boil. Stir in the pasta, and simmer until pasta is al dente, about 20 minutes. Remove from heat, stir in ¼ cup Pecorino Romano cheese. Let rest for a few minutes, covered. Serve with additional grated cheese on the side.

Minestra Rustica
GARBANZO BEAN AND WHOLE-WHEAT PASTA SOUP

SERVES 4

*O*ur use of whole-wheat pasta came as a spontaneous reaction to a nearly bare cupboard. It was surprising how well the flavors worked together. This soup cries out to be served in handmade pottery bowls because of the way the creamy golden beans look next to the reddish-brown pasta. The height of rustic simplicity.

1 *14-ounce can garbanzo beans or 1½ cups cooked garbanzo beans with liquid*

4 *cups water*

2 *cups imported whole-wheat elbows or broken whole-wheat spaghetti*

Salt

3 *tablespoons extra-virgin olive oil, plus additional for drizzling on soup*

2 *generous sprigs fresh rosemary*

3 *garlic cloves, peeled and lightly crushed*

Freshly ground black pepper to taste

Combine the beans, bean liquid, and water in a soup pot and bring to a boil. Add the pasta and cook until al dente, adding salt to taste. Meanwhile, combine the extra-virgin olive oil, rosemary, and garlic in a small skillet and cook over gentle heat to release the aromas. Just before serving, pour the olive oil from the small skillet into the soup pot, straining out and discarding the rosemary and garlic. Stir well. Grind pepper over the soup. Drizzle a small amount of additional extra-virgin olive oil over the top of each serving.

Minestra del Bosco

FOREST SOUP

*T*his fragrant, woodsy soup is perfect for a cold, wintry day. The thin strands of golden pasta look beautiful floating in their bath of richly flavored broth.

1 *ounce dried porcini mushrooms*	*Salt and freshly ground black pepper to taste*
Warm water	½ *pound imported capellini*
1½ *quarts beef broth*	*Freshly grated Parmesan cheese*
2 *tablespoons extra-virgin olive oil*	
½ *pound fresh mushrooms, wiped clean and sliced*	

Put the porcini mushrooms in a small bowl of warm water to cover and soak for 20 minutes or until tender. Remove the porcini from soaking liquid and reserve the soaking liquid. Rinse the porcini under cold water and coarsely chop. Strain the soaking liquid through cheesecloth or paper towels. Combine the porcini, strained soaking liquid, beef broth, and extra-virgin olive oil in a large pot and bring to a boil. Add the fresh mushrooms, salt, and pepper. When the soup returns to a boil, break the pasta in half and add to the pot. Cook at a boil until al dente. Place a few tablespoons of Parmesan cheese in the bottom of a soup tureen. Add the soup and stir. Correct seasonings. Serve with extra Parmesan cheese.

Minestrone Verde

ALL-GREEN MINESTRONE

SERVES 6 TO 8

This soup is a beautiful monochromatic study in green, with the fresh flavors of vegetables and herbs. The pesto sauce should be added right before serving. Pesto's flavor and aroma are released when it first comes into contact with the heat of the soup. This minestrone is also delicious served at room temperature.

1 *bunch leeks, 2 to 3*
¼ *cup extra-virgin olive oil*
2–3 *garlic cloves, peeled and minced*
1 *onion, peeled and thinly sliced*
½ *cabbage, finely shredded*
Water
½ *pound fresh small, tender green beans or haricots verts, trimmed and washed*
3–4 *small, firm zucchini, trimmed and sliced*

Handful chopped Italian parsley
5–10 *leaves fresh basil, coarsely chopped*
½–1 *cup imported conchigliette*
2 *cups fresh or frozen peas*
Salt and freshly ground black pepper to taste
2 *tablespoons Pesto Sauce (see page 92)*
Freshly grated Parmesan cheese

Make two vertical cuts lengthwise in the leeks to expose the layers, and wash thoroughly under cold running water. Drain and coarsely chop. Heat the extra-virgin olive oil in a soup pot. Add the garlic, onion, and leeks. Cook over moderate heat for 2 minutes, stirring frequently. Add the cabbage, stir, and cover pan. Cook covered until cabbage begins to wilt. Add water to cover by 2 inches and bring to a boil. Turn the heat down and simmer until cabbage is tender. Add the green beans or haricots verts, zucchini, parsley, and basil and simmer until vegetables are barely done. Add the pasta and continue cooking until it is al dente. Add the peas at the last minute. Add salt and pepper. Serve immediately or at room temperature. Before serving, stir 1 teaspoon of pesto into each individual soup bowl. Pass extra pesto and Parmesan cheese.

TUTTO AL CRUDO

Pasta with Raw Sauces

*T*his is a very special category of pasta that uses the freshest and least traditional sauces of all. The only cooking required is boiling the water for the pasta. These pasta dishes are among the most healthful because of the raw extra-virgin olive oil and vegetables, which are cooked only by the heat of the pasta. In Italy these dishes are sometimes referred to as *pasta estiva,* an evocative term that brings to mind summer vacations and carefree holidays.

These brilliantly colored pasta dishes carry the scent of a garden in the warm sun. They make lavish use of ripe tomatoes, summer herbs, and tangy olives, anchovies, and capers. Excellent for the most effortless eating on hot summer days, lazy days, days at the beach, or on a shaded terrace.

Although many of these dishes are appropriate for summer menus, some can be eaten all year round, such as Maccheroncini alla Campagnola (see page 90), where summer produce is not the main focus.

Spaghetti al Sugo di Limone
SPAGHETTI WITH TOMATO-LEMON SAUCE

SERVES 4 TO 6

*U*nlike many dishes in this chapter that can be eaten at room temperature, this one must be eaten immediately while the pasta is hot. It makes use of raw tomatoes in a very fresh pure way. If you grow your own tomatoes, pick them before they are fully mature. All over Italy these tomatoes are served raw in salads. They have a snappy, tart yet sweet crunch to them that works really well in this sauce. Avoid the pink tomatoes, those otherwordly kinds that are neither ripe nor green but fall into a twilight zone somewhere in between.

2 *pounds fresh tomatoes, preferably Roma, ripe but firm*
Salt and freshly ground black pepper

1 *pound imported spaghetti*
Juice of 1 large lemon
6 *tablespoons extra-virgin olive oil*

Cut the tomatoes in half and remove the seeds and excess liquid. Trim the stem ends and cut tomato halves into small dice. Place in a large pasta serving bowl. Sprinkle with a generous amount of salt and pepper. Meanwhile, cook spaghetti in abundant boiling salted water until al dente. Drain well and add to the serving bowl. Dress with the lemon juice and extra-virgin olive oil. Mix well and serve immediately.

Pasta Santa Caterina

SERVES 4 TO 6

This pasta is served at the Hotel Santa Caterina in Amalfi. It is but one variation on the most popular summer pasta, tossed with fresh raw tomato and herbs. Here it is marinated with extra-virgin olive oil, basil, parsley, dried oregano, and grated Parmesan cheese. Use Greek oregano rather than the Mexican kind. The Greek variety, commonly used in Italian cooking, is more perfumed and less assertive in flavor.

Late spring is a particularly special time of the year to visit Amalfi. Flowers are in bloom, and the light misty rain keeps everything green and moist, and the air is full of the candy-sweet scent of irises.

2 *pounds ripe tomatoes, peeled, seeded, and cut into small dice*

6 *tablespoons extra-virgin olive oil*

1 *teaspoon dried oregano*

2 *tablespoons chopped Italian parsley*

2 *tablespoons chopped fresh basil*

1 *large garlic clove, peeled and minced*

3 *tablespoons freshly grated Parmesan cheese, plus additional for table use*

Salt and freshly ground black pepper to taste

1 *pound imported spaghetti*

In a medium bowl combine all the ingredients, except the pasta. Marinate for about 1 hour at room temperature. Cook the pasta in abundant boiling salted water until al dente. Drain thoroughly. Transfer the pasta to a heated serving dish. Add the sauce and toss. Adjust the seasonings and serve with extra Parmesan cheese on the side.

Summer Salsa Forte
STRONG SUMMER SAUCE

SERVES 4 TO 6

An uncooked version of the piquant and spicy puttanesca sauce, one of the most loved of all Roman sauces. In our recipe the juices turn dark red and rich tasting after the ingredients are marinated, thanks to the olives and anchovies. Tomatoes and Italian parsley brighten those strong, salty flavors. Serve this dish on a lazy summer day with cool wine. End with a basket of fresh figs for dessert.

2 *pounds ripe tomatoes, peeled, seeded, and cut into small dice*

4 *anchovies, chopped to a paste*

½ *cup pitted oil-cured black olives, coarsely chopped*

3 *tablespoons small capers*

1 *bunch Italian parsley, leaves chopped*

2 *garlic cloves, peeled and minced*

½ *teaspoon red chile pepper flakes*

Salt to taste

½ *cup extra-virgin olive oil*

1 *pound imported cavatappi*

Freshly grated Parmesan cheese

In a small bowl combine all the ingredients, except the pasta and grated cheese. Marinate at room temperature for 30 minutes to 1 hour. Cook the pasta in abundant boiling salted water until al dente. Quickly drain and toss with the sauce. Serve immediately with Parmesan cheese on the side.

Spaghetti alla Checca

SUMMER SPAGHETTI

SERVES 4 TO 6

This sauce is synonymous with summer in Italy. Ripe flavorful tomatoes, sweet-smelling basil, and pure white mozzarella are the ingredients that signal summer.

5 large red ripe tomatoes, stems removed, cut into small dice	Salt and freshly ground black pepper to taste
1–2 garlic cloves, peeled and finely diced	1–1½ cups extra-virgin olive oil
5–6 leaves fresh basil, coarsely chopped	4–6 ounces fresh mozzarella in water, cut into small dice
	1 pound imported spaghetti

In a medium bowl combine the tomatoes, garlic, basil, salt, and pepper. Add enough of the extra-virgin olive oil to just cover tomato mixture. Marinate at room temperature for at least 1 hour, preferably 2 or 3. Drain the mozzarella, place in a pasta serving bowl, and allow to come to room temperature. Cook the pasta in abundant boiling salted water until it is al dente. Quickly drain and immediately pour the pasta over the mozzarella in the serving bowl. Toss at once to enable the heat of the pasta to melt the cheese, then add the tomato mixture and mix well.

Conchiglie della Spiaggia
BEACH PASTA

SERVES 4 TO 6

*T*he briny flavors of this dish remind us of fortunate summers spent lazing beside Mediterranean waters.

5 *large red ripe tomatoes, stems removed, cut into small dice*	1–2 *anchovy fillets, finely chopped*
6–10 *leaves fresh basil, coarsely chopped*	*Salt and freshly ground black pepper to taste*
2 *6½-ounce cans tuna packed in oil, flaked with fork*	½–1 *cup extra-virgin olive oil*
¼–½ *cup pitted black Kalamata or Gaeta olives*	1 *pound imported medium pasta shells*

In a medium bowl combine the tomatoes, basil, tuna, olives, anchovies, salt, and pepper. Add enough of the extra-virgin olive oil to just cover mixture. Stir and let the sauce marinate at room temperature for at least 1 hour. If the sauce is made ahead, it is not necessary to refrigerate it. Leave it in a cool, shady spot in the kitchen. If you feel more comfortable letting the sauce marinate in the refrigerator, take it out at least 1 hour before cooking the pasta to bring it to room temperature. Cook the pasta in abundant boiling salted water until al dente. Quickly drain and transfer to a shallow serving bowl. Add the sauce and mix well.

Perciatelli alle Sarde

*T*his uncooked sauce explodes with flavor as it takes its cue from the famous Sicilian specialty Pasta con le Sarde (see page 174). Look for the very round female bulbs of fennel. They are much sweeter than the flat male bulbs. This pasta is equally delicious hot or at room temperature.

2 *cans boneless sardines packed in olive oil, drained*

2 *bulbs fennel, cut into thin julienne*

¼ *cup minced wild fennel tops or reserved feathery tops from bulb fennel*

2 *anchovy fillets, minced*

1 *tablespoon chives, minced*

2 *tablespoons pine nuts, lightly toasted*

2 *tablespoons golden raisins, plumped in hot water*

Juice of 1 lemon

1 *cup extra-virgin olive oil*

Salt to taste

Pinch of red chile pepper flakes

Pinch of saffron threads, soaked in 2 tablespoons warm water

1 *pound imported perciatelli, broken into 3-inch lengths*

Combine all ingredients except pasta in a medium mixing bowl. Let marinate, preferably at room temperature, for at least 4 hours. If refrigeration is necessary, remove from the refrigerator and bring back to room temperature at least 1 hour before serving. Cook the pasta in abundant boiling salted water until it is al dente. Quickly drain and place in shallow serving bowl. Toss with sardine-fennel mixture.

Linguine Fini alla Rughetta

THIN LINGUINE WITH ARUGOLA AND SPICY TOMATO SAUCE

SERVES 4 TO 6

All the rage during a recent summer visit to Italy. The pepperiness of the arugola is enhanced by the spiciness of the cayenne.

5 *large red ripe tomatoes, peeled and seeded*

2 *large bunches arugola, stems removed, washed and dried*

Pinch of ground cayenne or 2 whole cayenne peppers

Salt to taste

¼ *cup extra-virgin olive oil*

1 *pound imported linguine fini*

Freshly grated Parmesan cheese

Roughly chop the tomatoes and pass them through the coarse disk of a food mill into a medium bowl. Finely chop the arugola and add it to the tomato puree. If using cayenne powder, add it to the tomatoes with salt and extra-virgin olive oil. Stir to mix. Let the sauce sit at room temperature for at least 1 hour to allow the flavors to mix. Bring abundant salted water to the boil. If using whole cayenne peppers, add them to the boiling water. Cook the pasta in the vigorously boiling water until al dente. Drain immediately and carefully remove the whole cayenne peppers. Transfer the pasta to a shallow serving bowl and add the sauce. Toss and serve immediately. Pass Parmesan cheese.

Spaghetti Simonetta

A recipe from Simonetta, an Italian postwar fashion designer who had her own couture house in Paris. This stylish denizen of the world of high fashion wrote a fascinating little cookbook, *A Snob in the Kitchen,* published in 1967, that has been a source of constant inspiration. Fun, chic, and full of wonderful food sense. This recipe is one of her creations. If you wish, substitute 1½ pounds fresh Pasta allo Zafferano (see page 34), cut into tonnarelli, for the saffron and dried spaghetti.

Salt

1 teaspoon saffron

1 pound imported spaghetti

3 tablespoons unsalted butter, softened at room temperature

2 garlic cloves, peeled and minced

Freshly ground black pepper to taste

Freshly grated Parmesan cheese

To cook pasta, bring a large pot of water to a boil. Add the salt and saffron. When the water returns to the boil, add the spaghetti. Meanwhile, place the butter, garlic, and a few tablespoons of Parmesan in a serving bowl. When the pasta is al dente, drain, leaving a little of the cooking water clinging to the strands. Add to the serving bowl. Toss, adding a little salt to taste. Serve with additional grated Parmesan cheese at the table.

Fettuccine al Burro e Parmigiano

SERVES 4 TO 6

*U*nsalted butter that is softened at room temperature has a light, fresh flavor which gives this dish its character. Add extra flavor and elegance to this simple dish by using fresh pasta made with herbs (page 35).

1 *stick unsalted butter, softened at room temperature*
1 *cup freshly grated Parmesan cheese, plus additional for table use*

Freshly ground black pepper
1 *pound fresh fettuccine or 1 recipe Pasta all'Uovo I or II (see pages 32–33), cut into fettuccine*

Break up the butter into a few pieces and place in a serving dish. Add the grated Parmesan cheese right on top of the butter. Do not stir them together. Meanwhile, cook the fettuccine in abundant boiling salted water just until tender. Drain thoroughly and place in a serving bowl. Toss with the butter and Parmesan. Add pepper to taste. Pass extra Parmesan cheese.

Raw Summer Sauce with Mozzarella

A bouquet of summer colors and flavors. This is as close as we get to advocating pasta salad. The addition of oregano and red chile pepper accents the sweetness of the summer vegetables. The hot pasta very lightly cooks the small, diced ingredients, releasing flavor and aroma. Tubetti, shaped like short tubes, echo the small dice of the vegetables and fresh cheese.

1 *pound ripe tomatoes, cut into small dice*

1 *yellow pepper, seeds and membranes removed, cut into small dice*

2 *small zucchini, trimmed and cut into small dice*

½ *hothouse cucumber, peeled, seeded, and cut into small dice*

1 *tender carrot, peeled and thinly sliced*

1 *small red onion, finely diced*

1 *bunch fresh basil leaves, chopped*

Dried oregano to taste

1 *pound imported tubetti*

½ *teaspoon minced fresh red chile pepper*

Salt

6 *tablespoons extra-virgin olive oil*

¾ *pound fresh mozzarella, diced*

Freshly grated Parmesan or Pecorino Romano cheese

Combine the chopped vegetables and the herbs in a serving bowl. Cook the tubetti in abundant boiling salted water until al dente. Drain and transfer to the serving bowl containing the other ingredients. Add the red chile pepper, salt, and extra-virgin olive oil, and toss. Sprinkle with the mozzarella, toss again, and serve with grated cheese on the side.

Spaghetti al Caprino
SPAGHETTI WITH GOAT CHEESE AND TOMATO

Goat cheese is almost chalky in texture, and it combines richness with a lemony tang that keeps it from becoming too heavy. Here it melts into a light, fresh mixture of tomato, basil, and extra-virgin olive oil, adding a touch of creaminess to the finished sauce.

1½ *pounds tomatoes, preferably Roma*	*Salt to taste*
1 *bunch fresh basil*	4 *ounces fresh goat cheese*
6 *tablespoons extra-virgin olive oil*	1 *pound imported spaghetti*

Cut the tomatoes in half horizontally, and remove the seeds. Cut tomato halves into very small dice. Chop the basil coarsely. Combine the tomatoes, basil, extra-virgin olive oil, and salt in a large pasta bowl. Crumble the goat cheese into small pieces and add to the bowl. Meanwhile, cook the pasta in a large pot of boiling salted water. When tender but al dente, drain well and add to the pasta bowl. Toss quickly and serve immediately.

Maccheroncini alla Campagnola

We include this dish here rather than in the cheese chapter because of its simple, uncomplicated spirit. The sauce is rich, tangy, and hot from fresh red chile pepper and raw garlic. Fresh firm white garlic is essential when used raw, as it is here, to produce a strong, fresh flavor. This pasta looks at home in a big earthenware pasta bowl. Serve platters of lightly cooked vegetables as a second course, and a cool, dry red wine.

⅛ *pound firm ricotta salata*
1 *small fresh red chile pepper*
1 *very fresh large garlic clove, peeled*
Small bunch Italian parsley
Salt

1 *pound imported sedanini or other short pasta*
⅓ *cup finely chopped oil-cured black olives (about 12–14)*
½ *cup extra-virgin olive oil*

Grate the ricotta salata and set aside. Finely chop together the red chile pepper and garlic. Separately, chop the parsley. Cook the pasta in abundant boiling salted water. When the pasta is al dente, drain well and place in a warm serving dish. Sprinkle with the chopped olives, red chile pepper, garlic, parsley, and grated ricotta salata. Mix to distribute evenly. Combine with the extra-virgin olive oil and mix again.

Pesto of Sun-dried Tomatoes
with Arugola

*D*rying tomatoes in the summer sun to preserve them for the cold winter months is an old Italian country tradition. It is a shame that when a food suddenly becomes "in," a lack of understanding of its function in relation to taste and texture causes it to be used indiscriminately. The sun-dried tomato has suffered such a fate. Use sun-dried tomatoes that you make yourself. (See recipe on page 276 in *Cucina Fresca*.) They must have enough moisture left in them to create the creamy consistency required for this sauce. What results is a crimson paste, reminiscent of old-fashioned homemade *concentrata*, the true tomato paste.

¾ *cup plump, moist sun-dried tomatoes*

1 *small garlic clove*

½ *teaspoon red chile pepper flakes*

¼ *cup extra-virgin olive oil*

Salt

1 *pound imported spaghettini*

2 *bunches arugola, trimmed and coarsely chopped*

Freshly grated Parmesan cheese

In a food processor with a steel blade or in a blender, process the sun-dried tomatoes with the garlic, red chile pepper, and extra-virgin olive oil until mixture has a rough pesto texture. Scrape out the mixture and transfer to a small bowl, and add salt to taste. Cook the spaghettini in abundant boiling salted water until al dente. Drain, leaving a little water clinging to the strands. Place pasta in a heated serving bowl and toss with pesto to coat lightly. Sprinkle with the chopped arugola, toss again, and serve with Parmesan cheese on the side.

Linguine al Pesto

SERVES 4 TO 6

*P*esto is the classic uncooked sauce. It has become very popular and justifiably so. Rich and intense in flavor, pesto is always diluted with a little pasta water when served. Only fresh, fragrant basil should be used. Other ingredients, such as parsley, are not traditional. In this recipe potatoes and green beans, classic Genoese additions, are cooked with the pasta and throw into relief the richness of the pesto. Along the Italian Riviera, pesto country, the indefinably sweet smell of basil perfumes the air just as rosemary does in Tuscany on a hot, clear day.

- 2 *cups fresh basil, stems removed*
- 4 *garlic cloves, peeled*
- ¼ *cup toasted pine nuts*
- ⅓ *cup extra-virgin olive oil, divided*
- ½ *cup freshly grated Parmesan cheese, plus additional for table use*

- ¼ *pound small, fresh tender green beans or haricots verts, trimmed*
- 1 *russet potato, peeled and diced*
- 1 *pound imported linguine*
- *Salt and freshly ground black pepper to taste*

To make pesto, place the basil leaves, garlic cloves, and pine nuts in a food processor with a steel blade. Process until basil and garlic are finely chopped. With machine running, add half the extra-virgin olive oil in a slow, steady stream. Turn off processor and add ½ cup Parmesan cheese. Again, process until the cheese is absorbed. With the machine running slowly, add the remaining oil. When the pesto is creamy, add salt and pepper. Use immediately or top with a thin layer of olive oil to prevent the basil from turning dark, and store in a tightly closed container.

To finish the pasta dish, bring a large pot of salted water to the boil. Add the diced potato to the boiling water. Cook for 5 minutes. Add the green beans and pasta to the potatoes cooking in boiling water. While the pasta is cooking, place the pesto in a shallow serving bowl. Cook all until pasta is al dente, at which time the vegetables should be properly cooked. Drain in a colander, reserving some pasta water. Transfer the cooked pasta, green beans, and potato to the serving bowl containing the pesto, and toss. Add 1 to 2 tablespoons of cooking water, if necessary, to enable the pesto to coat the pasta. Serve immediately and pass extra Parmesan cheese.

Pasta Strascinata
PASTA SAUTÉED WITH HERBS

SERVES 4 TO 6

*I*n the spirit of raw sauces, *strascinata* is literally translated as "being dragged." Here, the warm herbs and hot pasta are "dragged" or tossed together in a pan over heat to help the pasta take on the aromatic properties of the herbs. It is important to slightly undercook the pasta so that it doesn't soften during its second brief cooking.

6 *tablespoons extra-virgin olive oil*

2 *tablespoons unsalted butter*

3 *garlic cloves, peeled and minced*

Red chile pepper flakes to taste

Bunch chopped Italian parsley

2 *bunches fresh basil, leaves coarsely chopped*

4 *sprigs fresh mint, leaves coarsely chopped*

2 *sprigs fresh rosemary, leaves finely chopped*

Salt and freshly ground black pepper to taste

1 *pound imported conchiglie*

Freshly grated Parmesan cheese

In a large sauté pan combine the extra-virgin olive oil, butter, garlic, and red chile pepper. Heat gently until the garlic begins to sizzle. Add the chopped herbs, salt, and pepper, and cook over low heat for 2 to 3 minutes. Cook the pasta in abundant boiling salted water. When the pasta is very al dente, drain well and add to the sauté pan with the herbs. Sauté quickly over medium heat to coat the pasta. Sprinkle with grated Parmesan cheese, toss again, and correct the seasonings. Serve in a heated dish with additional Parmesan cheese on the side.

Spaghetti al Verde
SPAGHETTI WITH PIQUANT SAUCE
SERVES 4 TO 6

The ultimate sauce for lovers of vinegar and things piquant. Here ingredients are warmed to release the flavors. Strong and green, the sauce can be made when you have almost nothing in the pantry. To make Olio Santo, simply add 1 to 2 tablespoons of red chile flakes and a couple of bay leaves to a bottle of great extra-virgin olive oil. Marinate for 3 weeks before using.

½–1 *cup extra-virgin olive oil, divided*

2–3 *garlic cloves, peeled and minced*

2 *anchovy fillets, finely chopped*

1 *tablespoon capers, drained and coarsely chopped*

¼ *cup good-quality green olives in brine, pitted and quartered*

Large handful coarsely chopped Italian parsley

5–10 *fresh basil leaves, coarsely chopped*

Pinch of red chile pepper flakes

Salt, optional

1 *pound imported spaghetti*

Olio Santo

Heat half the extra-virgin olive oil in a small saucepan over moderate heat. Add the garlic and anchovies, and cook until the garlic begins to turn opaque and the anchovies fall apart. Add the capers, olives, parsley, basil, red chile flakes, and, if necessary, salt to taste. Cook just until the ingredients are coated with oil and aromas begin to rise. Remove from the heat and add the remaining oil. Let macerate for at least 15 minutes. Cook the spaghetti in abundant boiling salted water until al dente. Drain quickly and transfer to a shallow serving bowl. Pour warm oil-herb mixture over spaghetti and toss to mix well. Serve immediately. Pass Olio Santo.

Tagliarini dell'Orto

PASTA FROM THE KITCHEN GARDEN

*T*he butter smooths out the strong herbal flavors and helps marry the herbs to the pasta. Try your own combination of herbs, depending on what is in your garden or available in the market. Remember to use a tender, milder type, such as basil, as the main herb, and a stronger herb, such as chives, as an accent.

2 *cups fresh basil leaves*

5 *sprigs fresh marjoram, leaves only*

1 *sprig fresh thyme, leaves only*

½ *cup extra-virgin olive oil*

2 *garlic cloves, peeled and coarsely chopped*

¼ *cup pine nuts*

3 *tablespoons softened unsalted butter*

½ *cup freshly grated Parmesan cheese*

Salt

1 *pound fresh tagliarini or 1 recipe Pasta all'Uovo I or II (see pages 32–33), cut into tagliarini*

¼ *pound prosciutto, cut into julienne*

Freshly ground black pepper to taste

In a blender, or a food processor with steel blade, combine the basil, marjoram, thyme, extra-virgin olive oil, garlic, and pine nuts. Blend until a rough paste forms. Scrape the mixture out of the blender and transfer to a small bowl. Blend in butter and Parmesan cheese, using a wooden spoon.

Season with salt to taste. Cook the pasta in abundant boiling salted water until al dente. Drain quickly, reserving some of the pasta water. Toss the pasta with the herb pesto, adding a little of the hot cooking water to thin the sauce. Sprinkle the prosciutto over the pasta and top with freshly ground black pepper.

PASTA DELLA LATTERIA

Pasta Dishes from the Dairy — Yogurt to Gorgonzola

*T*here is a wide range of dairy foods that are staples in the repertoire of ingredients used with pasta: The mild, melting quality of fresh or smoked mozzarella merges beautifully with pasta, the strands of cheese creating a delectable tangle. Ricotta is a light, fresh, soft cheese used with pasta alone or in combination with vegetables or meats. Its soft quality and almost neutral flavor are welcome in many pasta dishes. Ricotta salata is a firmer version that is salted to remove excess water, it adds a stronger flavor to pasta sauces. Yogurt is a modern addition to the list of dairy products in Italian cooking. It has an appealing light, tart flavor, and its smooth texture coats the strands of pasta perfectly. Mascarpone, the richest of the soft cheeses, is similar to American cream cheese, but has a texture and delicacy closer to heavy whipped cream. It must be eaten soon after it is made or it will spoil. Because it melts quickly to form a sauce, mascarpone is often used instead of butter or cream to cloak pasta. It has a fresh buttery taste that goes well with fruits and desserts. Sweet, unsalted butter is always used. There is no doubt about its freshness. Perfectly ripened Gorgonzola cheese is another glory of the Italian *latticini,* dairy products. When Gorgonzola is at its peak of ripeness, it is sweet, creamy, and tangy all at once, and has the ability to melt in contact with the heat of the pasta. Fresh cream is not used very often in Italian sauces. It is used mostly in northern Italy, but only in small amounts and quickly reduced.

Nothing is more appealing than a cheese shop in Italy with its heady aromas of rich milk and aged cheese, reminiscent of pastures, grasses, and wild flowers: fresh balls of mozzarella floating in a milky bath, pure white ricotta, golden Parmesan cheese, and cream and silver-blue–streaked Gorgonzola. These cheese shops are found all over Italy, with each region offering its own unique varieties based on the land and climate. The cheeses we use in these recipes should be available either in specialty cheese shops or at your local Italian market. Look for locally made fresh and smoked mozzarella, ricotta, and mascarpone.

Salsa Rosa con Vodka

One of the trendy Italian sauces, fast becoming a classic. A perfect pasta dish for a New Year's Eve celebration, followed by fresh cracked crab and ending with Espresso Jelly from *Cucina Fresca* (see pages 258–259).

2 tablespoons unsalted butter

1 tablespoon extra-virgin olive oil

3 small dried red chile peppers, crushed

¼ cup vodka

2 cups imported canned Italian tomatoes, seeded and pureed

Salt and freshly ground black pepper to taste

¼ cup cream

1 pound imported gnocchetti rigati

Freshly grated Parmesan cheese

Combine the butter, extra-virgin olive oil, and chile peppers in a sauté pan. Cook over low heat for 2 to 3 minutes. Add the vodka, turn heat to medium high, and let the vodka boil briskly for several minutes. Add the pureed tomatoes, salt, and pepper, and cook over medium heat until sauce thickens, about 10 minutes. Reduce the heat to low and slowly stir in cream. Continue to cook over low heat for several minutes, correct the seasonings, and turn off heat. Meanwhile, cook the pasta in abundant boiling salted water until al dente. Drain well, transfer to serving dish, and combine with the sauce. Add a generous sprinkling of Parmesan cheese, toss again, and serve with additional grated cheese on the side.

Pasta al Limone

*T*his sauce features an unusual pairing of anchovies and cream. The onion and lemon fill the notes in between.

2 *tablespoons extra-virgin olive oil*

1 *tablespoon unsalted butter*

10 *anchovy fillets*

1 *large onion, finely diced*

Juice of 1 large lemon and lemon zest, finely minced

1 *cup cream*

3 *slices lemon*

1 *pound imported spaghetti*

Salt

2 *tablespoons chopped Italian parsley*

Cook the extra-virgin olive oil, butter, and anchovies in a medium sauté pan over low heat for a few minutes until anchovies dissolve. Add the onion and cook over low heat until the onion softens, about 20 minutes. Add the lemon juice and lemon zest and cook for an additional 5 minutes. Stir in the cream and cook over very low heat until the cream thickens. Meanwhile, combine the lemon slices and a generous amount of water in a pasta cooking pot. Bring to a boil. Add salt and when water returns to a boil, add the spaghetti and cook until al dente. Drain well and toss with the sauce. Correct the seasonings. Sprinkle with parsley.

Lemon and Black Olive Sauce
with Fettuccine

*I*n this lightest of all cream sauces, the fresh cream is not reduced, but tossed with the cooked fettuccine over a flame just until the liquid is absorbed by the pasta. The lemon flavor should be quite pronounced. The olives add their special suave flavor and black gloss.

1 *cup cream*

Finely chopped zest of 2 lemons

1 *pound fresh fettuccine or 1 recipe Pasta all'Uovo I or II (see pages 32–33), cut into fettuccine*

3 *tablespoons unsalted butter*

15 *oil-cured black olives, pitted and very coarsely chopped*

2 *tablespoons chopped Italian parsley*

Salt and freshly ground black pepper to taste

Freshly grated Parmesan cheese

Combine the cream and lemon zest in a small bowl. Cover with plastic wrap and refrigerate for several hours. Remove from refrigerator and let return to room temperature. Cook the pasta in abundant boiling salted water. When the pasta is very al dente, drain well. Add the butter to the pot in which you cook the pasta, return the pasta to the pot, and toss it with the butter. Add the cream and lemon zest and toss again over medium heat to reduce the cream. Sprinkle with the olives, parsley, salt, pepper, and a little Parmesan cheese. Toss again. Serve with more grated cheese on the side.

Fettuccine with Prosciutto

The citrus flavors are released as they come in contact with the hot fettuccine. The egg and cream mixture turns into a velvety light coating that is absorbed beautifully by the porous tender pasta. Buy good-quality prosciutto that is pink and buttery, not dark and excessively salty.

2 *egg yolks*

1 *cup cream*

½ *cup freshly grated Parmesan cheese, plus additional for table use*

Zest of ½ orange

Zest of ½ lemon

Salt and freshly ground black pepper

1 *pound fresh fettuccine or 1 recipe Pasta all'Uovo I or II (see pages 32–33), cut into fettuccine*

¼ *pound prosciutto, cut into julienne*

In a large serving bowl combine the egg yolks, cream, ½ cup Parmesan cheese, orange and lemon zests, and salt and pepper to taste. Beat slightly and set aside in a warm place. Cook the fettuccine in abundant boiling salted water, just until tender. Drain well and add to the serving bowl. Toss the pasta with the egg and cream mixture, and add the prosciutto and additional salt and pepper to taste. Serve with Parmesan cheese on the side.

Spaghetti alla Carbonara

SERVES 4 TO 6

*T*he ultimate creamy carbonara sauce, this is a rich variation on a classic staple of every trattoria in Rome. Best served as the centerpiece of a meal, followed by a simple tart green salad.

¼ *pound pancetta, thinly sliced*

2 *tablespoons extra-virgin olive oil*

1 *tablespoon unsalted butter*

3 *garlic cloves, peeled and crushed*

1 ½ *teaspoons red chile pepper flakes*

1 *pound imported spaghetti*

4 *egg yolks*

¼ *cup cream*

¼ *cup freshly grated Pecorino Romano cheese*

½ *cup freshly grated Parmesan cheese*

Freshly ground black pepper

Finely chopped Italian parsley

Cut the pancetta into thin strips. Combine the extra-virgin olive oil, butter, garlic, red chile pepper, and pancetta, and sauté over low heat until the pancetta renders its fat. Take off heat and remove the garlic cloves. Cook the spaghetti in abundant boiling salted water until al dente. While the spaghetti is cooking, lightly beat the egg yolks and combine them with the cream, grated cheeses, pancetta, and its fat. Drain the spaghetti and add to a heated serving dish. Season with plenty of black pepper and sprinkle with parsley. Toss and serve immediately.

Capellini al Pomodoro e Panna
CAPELLINI WITH TOMATO AND CREAM

SERVES 4 TO 6

Amodern pasta, this combination of tomatoes and cream is often referred to as salsa rosa. A creamy pasta that's not really a cream sauce, one for those who find cream just too rich. The small amount of cream neutralizes any acidity in the tomatoes. The result is a smooth sauce with the mellow taste of cheese and the fragrance of basil that clings beautifully to the thin pasta.

1 *28-ounce can imported Italian tomatoes*

6 *tablespoons unsalted butter, divided*

8–10 *fresh basil leaves*

½ *cup heavy cream*

Scant ¼ *cup freshly grated Parmesan cheese*

Scant ¼ *cup freshly grated Pecorino Romano cheese*

Salt and freshly ground black pepper to taste

1 *pound imported capellini*

Lift the tomatoes out of their juice and pass through the medium disk of a food mill, or puree in a food processor. Melt 4 tablespoons of butter over low heat in a heavy medium skillet. Add the tomato puree and basil. Cook over medium-high heat until the tomato puree thickens. Add the cream and Parmesan and Pecorino cheeses, and continue cooking until sauce is fairly thick. Add salt and pepper. Cook the pasta in abundant boiling salted water until al dente. Quickly drain and transfer to shallow serving bowl. Toss pasta with remaining 2 tablespoons of butter. Add the tomato-cream mixture and toss. Serve immediately. Pass extra Parmesan cheese.

PASTA DISHES FROM THE DAIRY

Penne Piccoline con Radicchio

TINY PENNE WITH RADICCHIO CREAM SAUCE

SERVES 4 TO 6

We sampled this dish in a Roman restaurant, Grotte del Teatro di Pompeo, which included on its menu specialties from Treviso, the owner's hometown in northern Italy. The sauce was a subtle blend of slightly bitter radicchio, hot red chile pepper, and sweet cream. After the meal the owner brought out his own special reserve of homemade grappa with marinated apples and offered it, strong and tonic, as a fitting ending. Try to find the tiny penne piccoline, which are pretty and delicate-looking.

¼ cup extra-virgin olive oil

1 large garlic clove, peeled and minced

2 small dried red chile peppers, crushed

2 heads radicchio, or 4 heads Belgian endive, trimmed and chopped

¼ cup imported Italian canned tomatoes, pureed

Salt and freshly ground black pepper to taste

1 cup cream

1 pound imported penne piccoline

1 tablespoon chopped Italian parsley

Freshly grated Parmesan cheese

Combine the extra-virgin olive oil, garlic, and red chile peppers in a large sauté pan. Sauté over low heat for 2 to 3 minutes. Add the radicchio or Belgian endive, mix in flavored oil, and cook over medium heat until soft. Add the pureed tomatoes, salt, and pepper, and cook until sauce thickens. Add the cream and simmer until liquid reduces to a sauce consistency.

Cook the pasta in abundant boiling salted water. When al dente, drain well and combine with the sauce. Sprinkle with a little of the Parmesan cheese and toss. Garnish with chopped parsley.

Fettuccine Bianco e Nero
BLACK AND WHITE FETTUCCINE

SERVES 4 TO 6

An elegant balance of earthiness and sophistication. In flavor, too, the elements are nicely matched — the rich neutral flavor of the cream is joined to the meaty saltiness of the olive paste. This is a good dish when you need to put a special meal together in a hurry. Serve with champagne.

3 *tablespoons unsalted butter*
3 *heaping tablespoons imported black olive paste*
1 *cup cream*

1 *pound fresh fettuccine or 1 recipe Pasta all'Uovo I or II (see pages 32–33), cut into fettuccine*
Freshly grated Parmesan cheese

In a small sauté pan melt the butter over low heat. Add the black olive paste and blend with the butter. Stir in the cream and cook until cream has reduced slightly. Cook the fettuccine in abundant boiling salted water until al dente. Quickly drain and toss with the sauce and a little of the Parmesan cheese. Serve with extra grated cheese on the side.

PASTA DISHES FROM THE DAIRY

Fettuccine Dorate con Zucca e Spinaci
FETTUCCINE WITH GOLDEN SAUCE

SERVES 4 TO 6

*T*he red squash and cream form a mild, sweet sauce that is a lovely pale shade of peachy gold. Spinach adds a fresh green note, and the light flavor of smoky pancetta permeates the whole. Smoked pancetta is a specially cured Italian meat almost impossible to find here. Substitute high-quality thick-cut bacon and you will achieve nearly the same result. A great pasta for a brisk fall day.

1 *pound red squash, such as banana or butternut*

1 *pound tender spinach, stems trimmed*

Salt

3 *tablespoons extra-virgin olive oil*

1 *small onion, finely diced*

¼ *pound smoked pancetta or bacon, cut into small strips*

1 ½ *cup cream*

Pinch of grated nutmeg

Salt and freshly ground black pepper

1 *pound fresh fettuccine or 1 recipe Pasta all'Uovo I or II (see pages 32–33), cut into fettuccine*

Unsalted butter

Freshly grated Parmesan cheese

Remove the seeds and fibers from the squash. Cut the squash into chunks and peel with a vegetable peeler. Place squash pieces in a baking dish, cover with foil, and bake in a preheated 350° oven for 40 minutes or until tender. Cool, put through a potato ricer or food mill, and set aside. Wash the spinach and cook it in a pot with just the water that clings to the leaves;

add salt to taste. When the spinach is tender, drain well in a colander. Chop coarsely and set aside. Combine the extra-virgin olive oil and onion in a large sauté pan and cook over low heat until onion softens, about 12 minutes. Add the pancetta and sauté until it colors but before it crisps. Add the chopped spinach and toss to flavor it. Add the squash puree, cream, and nutmeg, and black pepper to taste. Gently warm the ingredients over low heat. Cook the fettuccine in abundant boiling salted water until just tender. Quickly drain, leaving some water clinging to the strands of pasta. Transfer the fettuccine to a serving dish and toss in enough butter to coat lightly. Add the sauce and a sprinkling of grated Parmesan cheese. Toss, correct seasonings, and serve with a big bowl of Parmesan cheese at the table.

Lumachelle con Verdure e Panna

PASTA WITH GREEN VEGETABLES AND CREAM

SERVES 4 TO 6

*B*lanching the vegetables first brings out the bright green color. The preliminary cooking allows you to toss the vegetables with the cream quickly, thus keeping all the flavors fresh and light. This pasta dish, in shades of green and gold, has a special beauty.

5 *tablespoons unsalted butter, divided*

2 *garlic cloves, peeled and minced*

1 *ounce porcini mushrooms, soaked in warm water to cover for 20 minutes, drained, rinsed, and coarsely chopped*

½ *pound broccoli, stalks peeled, cut into ½-inch pieces, blanched*

½ *pound tender asparagus, stalks peeled, cut into ½-inch pieces, blanched*

1 *cup tender shelled peas, lightly cooked in a little salted water*

Salt and fresh ground black pepper to taste

1 *cup cream*

1 *bunch fresh basil, leaves coarsely chopped*

1 *pound imported lumachelle*

Freshly grated Parmesan cheese

Combine 4 tablespoons butter and the garlic in a large sauté pan. Cook over low heat for 2 to 3 minutes. Add the porcini mushrooms and toss in the flavored butter. Add the green vegetables, season with salt and pepper, and toss again. Add the cream and cook over high heat until cream reduces and thickens. Sprinkle with the basil and toss. Meanwhile, cook the lumachelle in abundant boiling salted water. Drain well and place in a serving bowl. Toss the pasta with the remaining butter. Add the sauce and a little Parmesan cheese and toss again. Serve with additional grated cheese on the side.

Penne al Gorgonzola

SERVES 4 TO 6

The sweet-rich tang of creamy *dolce latte* Gorgonzola is slightly tamed by the addition of ricotta and butter. Add plenty of coarsely ground fresh pepper for that special spicy aroma.

3 *ounces imported dolce latte Gorgonzola*

6 *ounces ricotta*

2 *tablespoons unsalted butter, softened at room temperature*

2 *tablespoons freshly grated Parmesan cheese, plus additional for table use*

Salt and freshly ground black pepper

1 *pound imported penne*

In a small bowl, and using a wooden spoon, beat together the Gorgonzola, ricotta, butter, Parmesan cheese, and salt and pepper to taste. Transfer to a shallow serving bowl. Cook the pasta in abundant boiling salted water until al dente. Add 2 to 3 tablespoons of pasta water to the cheese mixture and mix well. Drain the pasta and add immediately to the cheese mixture. Mix well and serve at once. Pass extra Parmesan cheese.

Fettuccine al Mascarpone

FRESH EGG PASTA WITH ITALIAN CREAM CHEESE

Mascarpone is a rich, fresh-tasting Italian cream cheese, lighter in texture than our cream cheese. Mascarpone is used in pasta sauces as well as in desserts, the most famous being tiramisù, a specialty that layers ladyfingers infused with coffee or chocolate with a mixture of creamy mascarpone. Here the cheese adds a rich flavor without the heaviness and cloying sweetness of a reduced heavy cream sauce.

2 tablespoons unsalted butter, softened at room temperature

4 ounces mascarpone

¼ cup freshly grated Parmesan cheese, plus additional for table use

12 fresh basil leaves

5 slices prosciutto, cut into thin slivers

Salt and freshly ground black pepper

1 pound fresh fettuccine or 1 recipe Pasta all'Uovo I or II (see pages 32–33), cut into fettuccine

Combine the butter and mascarpone in a bowl and beat with a wooden spoon. Add ¼ cup Parmesan cheese and mix well. Stack the basil leaves one on top of another and roll up like a cigar. Slice across the roll to create thin julienne strips of basil. Transfer the cheese mixture to a shallow serving bowl. Add the prosciutto, basil, salt, and pepper to taste. Cook the pasta in abundant boiling salted water until al dente. Quickly drain and add to the serving bowl containing the mascarpone mixture. Add the prosciutto and basil, and toss. Pass extra Parmesan cheese.

PASTA DELLA LATTERIA

Salsa Cremosa di Mascarpone e Pancetta Affumicata
CREAMY SAUCE WITH BACON

SERVES 4 TO 6

Mascarpone is the base for this sauce. The tomatoes tint it a pumpkin red, and the bacon adds its unique smokiness to this easy and delicious pasta.

1 *small onion, finely diced*

3 *tablespoons extra-virgin olive oil*

¼ *pound meaty smoked pancetta or thick-sliced bacon, cut into thin strips*

8 *canned imported tomatoes, about 1½ cups, seeded and pureed*

Salt

1 *pound fresh fettuccine or 1 recipe Pasta all'Uovo I or II (see pages 32–33), cut into fettuccine*

7 *ounces mascarpone*

12 *fresh basil leaves, cut into julienne*

In a large sauté pan cook onion in the extra-virgin olive oil over low heat until tender, about 10 to 12 minutes. Add the pancetta or bacon, raise the heat slightly, and cook until it colors but does not become crisp. Add the pureed tomatoes and a little salt, and let simmer until moisture evaporates. Meanwhile, cook the fettuccine in abundant salted boiling water until quite al dente. Drain, allowing some moisture to remain on the strands of pasta. Add the fettuccine to the sauce in the pan and toss over very low heat. Add the mascarpone and basil, and toss well.

Tonnarelli alla Gorgonzola

This classic creamy Gorgonzola sauce is also great on Potato Gnocchi (page 244). To make tonnarelli, roll out fresh egg pasta in thick sheets, then cut with finest blade to make a noodle similar to square spaghetti.

8 *tablespoons (1 stick) unsalted butter, cut into 8 pieces*

½ *pound imported dolce latte Gorgonzola, cut into small pieces*

1 *cup half-and-half or heavy cream, divided*

1 *pound fresh tonnarelli or 1 recipe Pasta all'Uovo II (see page 33), cut into tonnarelli*

½ *cup freshly grated Parmesan cheese, plus additional for table use*

Freshly ground black pepper to taste

Combine the butter, Gorgonzola, and half of the half-and-half or cream in a terra-cotta oven-to-table serving dish or in a heavy-bottomed saucepan. Heat over a low flame, stirring frequently, until the cheese melts and a slightly thick sauce forms. Keep warm while cooking the pasta. Cook the pasta in abundant salted boiling water until al dente. Quickly drain and add immediately to the serving dish or saucepan. Add the Parmesan cheese and the remaining half-and-half or heavy cream, and the freshly ground pepper. Toss over low heat just until mixed. Serve immediately. Pass extra Parmesan cheese.

Maccheroni Pastorale
PASTORAL MACARONI

Here is another sauce that is the essence of southern Italian sensibility, made with fresh ricotta, good pasta, a touch of enriching butter, with the grated Pecorino Romano cheese adding its distinctive stamp. Grilled lamb and roasted artichokes would fill out the meal, followed by a salad of bitter greens with chunks of a crisp tomato.

1 *pound imported sedanini*
1 *pound fresh ricotta*
3 *tablespoons unsalted butter, softened at room temperature*
Salt
Ground cayenne pepper to taste

Freshly ground black pepper to taste
Freshly grated Pecorino Romano cheese

Place a deep serving bowl and serving dishes in an oven set to low. Cook the pasta in abundant boiling salted water. A few minutes before the pasta is ready, remove the serving bowl from the oven, and in it mix together the ricotta, butter, salt, cayenne pepper, and a little black pepper. Stir in approximately 1/4 cup of the pasta cooking water to create a creamy sauce. Drain the pasta when al dente and toss with the sauce. Serve in heated pasta bowls with Pecorino Romano cheese on the side.

Rigatoni con Ricotta

SERVES 4 TO 6

A simple, rustic, homey dish served to us in a farmhouse kitchen near Rome. The ricotta was so fresh it was still warm.

- ¼ cup extra-virgin olive oil
- ½ small onion, peeled and finely diced
- 2 slices pancetta, coarsely chopped
- 1 pound ricotta
- Salt and freshly ground black pepper to taste
- ¼ cup freshly grated Parmesan cheese, plus additional for the table
- ¼ cup chopped Italian parsley
- 1 pound imported rigatoni

Heat the extra-virgin olive oil in a small heavy skillet. Add the onion and cook over low heat until it begins to soften. Add the pancetta and cook over medium heat until it renders its fat yet is not crisp. Remove from heat. Put onion-pancetta mixture, including all the fat, in a small mixing bowl. Add the ricotta, ¼ cup Parmesan cheese, parsley, salt, and pepper. Mix thoroughly with a wooden spoon. Start cooking the pasta in abundant boiling salted water. Place the ricotta mixture in a shallow serving bowl. Add to it 2 to 3 tablespoons of hot pasta water and mix well. When the pasta is al dente, quickly drain and add to the ricotta mixture in the serving bowl. Mix well and serve immediately. Pass extra Parmesan cheese.

Penne con Zucchini e Ricotta

SERVES 4 TO 6

This is an excellent example of how a simple combination of ingredients — small, tender zucchini and fresh ricotta — produces a dish that is light, nourishing, and delicious. Good ricotta is pure white, with a firm but moist texture that can be sliced like a cake.

1½ *pounds small, tender zucchini*
Salt
6 *tablespoons extra-virgin olive oil*
3 *garlic cloves, peeled and lightly crushed*
1 *pound imported penne rigate*

½ *pound fresh ricotta*
Freshly ground black pepper to taste
5 *large fresh basil leaves, coarsely chopped*

Trim the ends of the zucchini and slice into ¼-inch rounds. Sprinkle lightly with salt and set aside to drain on paper towels for about 1 hour. Dry well. Heat the extra-virgin olive oil in a large sauté pan. Cook the zucchini over medium heat until it is golden brown on both sides. Cook in batches, 1 layer at a time. Using a slotted spoon, transfer the zucchini to a plate and keep warm. Sauté the garlic cloves in the remaining olive oil until they are golden brown, remove from oil, and discard. Reserve the flavored oil. Cook the penne in abundant boiling salted water. When the penne are very al dente, reserve ¼ cup of the water and drain the pasta. Return the penne to the cooking pot, add the flavored oil, and toss. Add the ricotta, reserved cooking water, and pepper. Toss over low heat until the ricotta forms a sauce. Transfer the pasta to a heated platter, garnish with the zucchini rounds, and sprinkle with basil.

Whole-Wheat Fettuccine with Ricotta, Swiss Chard, and Prosciutto

Cooked greens are eaten with religious regularity in Italy. Swiss chard is so much a part of everyday meals, it is often simply called *verdura,* meaning "vegetable." It is served with good extra-virgin olive oil drizzled over the top, as a stuffing for fresh pasta, and, here, as part of a pasta sauce.

2 *pounds Swiss chard, stalks removed and reserved for another use*

Salt

8 *tablespoons (1 stick) unsalted butter, softened at room temperature, divided*

4 *slices prosciutto, diced*

1 *pound fresh whole-wheat fettuccine or 1 recipe Pasta Integrale (see page 33), cut into fettuccine*

½ *pound ricotta, at room temperature*

¾ *cup freshly grated Parmesan cheese*

Wash the chard leaves well. Cook in a sauté pan with the water that clings to the leaves and a little salt. When tender, drain and let cool. Press out the remaining moisture and chop not too finely. In a small sauté pan heat 4 tablespoons of butter and the diced prosciutto. Add the chard and toss well in the butter to flavor it. Cook the fettuccine in abundant boiling salted water. Meanwhile, transfer the chard to a warm serving dish and add to it the remaining butter, chopped chard, ricotta, and Parmesan cheese. Mix ingredients well. Right before pasta is done, add a little of the hot pasta water to the chard-ricotta mixture to create a creamy consistency. Drain the fettuccine when al dente, leaving a little water clinging to the strands. Add to the serving dish and toss quickly. Taste for salt, adding more if necessary.

Sugo di Magro
con Ricotta e Melanzane
LENTEN PASTA WITH RICOTTA
AND EGGPLANT

*T*he ingredients blend to create a creamy, satisfying Lenten pasta. Italy boasts an entire repertoire of meatless dishes for Lent called *al magro,* "the meager." In this traditional time of fasting and sacrifice, the Italians have risen to the occasion to create dishes of richness and variety despite the absence of meat.

Salt

1 *small eggplant, trimmed, cut into strips*

¼ *cup extra-virgin olive oil*

1 *small red onion, finely diced*

1 *tender carrot, finely chopped*

1 *stalk celery, strings removed, finely chopped*

½ *bunch Italian parsley, leaves finely chopped*

Small handful fresh basil leaves, chopped

1 *28-ounce can imported Italian tomatoes, seeded and pureed*

Salt and freshly ground black pepper to taste

¼ *pound fresh ricotta*

¼ *pound moist ricotta salata (see page 123)*

Extra-virgin olive oil for frying

1 *pound imported sedanini*

Freshly grated Parmesan cheese mixed with a few torn basil leaves

Salt the eggplant strips and let drain on paper towels for about 1 hour. In a sauté pan cook the extra-virgin olive oil, onion, carrot, celery, and herbs over low heat until softened. Add the pureed tomatoes, salt, and pepper. Raise the heat to medium and cook until sauce thickens. Mash together the ricotta and ricotta salata. Pat dry the eggplant strips. Heat the olive oil in a depth of ½ inch in a frying pan. When the oil is sizzling hot, add the eggplant and cook in small batches until golden. Drain on paper towels. Lightly salt the eggplant and keep it warm. Cook the pasta in abundant boiling salted water. Drain when al dente. Toss with the sauce and mashed ricotta cheeses. Add the eggplant and toss again. Check for salt and serve with basil-scented Parmesan cheese on the side.

Penne al Maestro

SERVES 4 TO 6

*T*his dish is a favorite of our friend the record producer. We've shared many late nights in Milan eating this pasta together when time and money were scarce.

1 *cup plain yogurt*
3 *egg yolks*
¾ *cup freshly grated Parmesan cheese, plus additional for table use*

Pinch of cinnamon
Salt and freshly ground black pepper to taste
1 *pound imported penne rigate*

In a pasta serving bowl beat together the yogurt, egg yolks, ¾ cup Parmesan cheese, cinnamon, salt, and pepper. Cook the penne in abundant boiling salted water until al dente. Quickly drain and add to the serving bowl. Gently toss the penne with the yogurt mixture. Serve immediately with extra Parmesan cheese on the side.

Maccheroni con Ricotta Salata

Ricotta salata is a cheese made from fresh sheep's milk and salted to draw out the water. Be sure you get moist ricotta salata rather than the drier, saltier type used for grating. This very simple rustic sauce requires only good extra-virgin olive oil and fresh pepper to make it complete. Adding anything else would interfere with the elemental quality of the finished product. It is a beautiful-looking dish with its golden pasta next to the chalk-white of the cheese — very pure.

1 *pound imported elbows*
½ *cup extra-virgin olive oil*
½ *pound moist ricotta salata*

Freshly ground black pepper
Freshly grated Pecorino
  Romano cheese

Cook the pasta in abundant boiling salted water. In a small sauté pan gently warm the extra-virgin olive oil. Crumble the ricotta salata into a warm serving dish. When pasta is al dente, drain, leaving some water clinging to it, and transfer to a serving dish. Pour the warmed olive oil over the pasta and toss. Sprinkle with lots of freshly ground pepper and serve with Pecorino Romano cheese on the side.

PASTA DISHES FROM THE DAIRY

Pasta del Giardino

Pasta from the Garden

*T*he Italian landscape is a checkerboard of farmland tucked between mountains in valleys and plains. A long growing season and agricultural expertise dating back to ancient times contribute to the important role vegetables play in Italian cooking. Never relegated to being an unimportant accompaniment to the main dish, vegetables have often been the mainstay of life for peasant families. Nowhere is this tradition more apparent than in combining pasta and vegetables to produce a dish. There is a poetry in the simplicity of this equation that reflects the connection with the seasons, the land, and its role in nourishing us. A bunch of wild greens or an apronful of tomatoes along with the pasta itself would be all that was needed to keep the wolf at bay. Often a sprinkling of cheese would add additional necessary nutrition. A touch of pancetta or some fresh garlic would provide the underpinnings for flavoring the dish. These dishes form a large part of the body of pasta recipes, and most clearly reflect everyday pasta eating habits. Although many may have their origins in *la cucina povera,* they were not the exclusive domain of the poor, but were eaten by the upper classes, too. By today's nutritional standards, these dishes represent the healthiest way to eat. Pasta with tender broccoli, with sweet zucchini, or with green beans all can be eaten again and again. The high quality of the vegetables keeps the recipes simple, and allows the natural flavors to shine through.

The markets of Italy reflect the quality and diversity of the vegetables grown. Under dappled light, beneath the shade of umbrellas, or in dark, cool shops are displayed the foods that remain such a vivid image for those who travel to Italy: big ridged tomatoes, creamy white eggplants streaked with mauve, potatoes with the warm smell of earth still on them, saffron-colored zucchini blossoms; the more subdued palette of the palest green fennel bulbs and gray-green artichokes with purple-tipped leaves; the brilliance of a thick slice of bright orange squash, and the magenta and white marbled radicchio. Each vegetable has its season and is awaited eagerly: the first tiny peas or tender asparagus of spring, the first scarlet peppers of summer, the porcini mushrooms of fall, dark and earthy.

If there is a real farmer's market in your area, that's the place to go to become acquainted with the seasons. You will also learn about the true tastes of vegetables, and that will become your standard for flavor and freshness. Many small farms are now growing foods organically, without chemicals that damage our health and affect flavor. Buy these organic vegetables when available. In the supermarket take a little extra time to select vegetables. A firm, glossy eggplant will be full of flesh rather than seeds. Bright green broccoli with tender stalks will taste sweet. Tomatoes that have a deep red color will make a full-bodied sauce. Supermarkets are responding to consumer demand and are stocking a much wider selection of vegetables. We hope this trend will continue and that we will be provided with better flavor, fewer pesticides, and even greater variety.

In this chapter are the pasta dishes that we both eat regularly, that are a basic part of our lives, and that sustain us.

PASTA FROM THE GARDEN

Penne al Pomodoro e Basilico
PENNE WITH SIMPLE TOMATO-BASIL SAUCE

The most basic of cooked sauces and the simplest, it is the benchmark of a good Italian home cook. It should be cooked fast and hot for the tomatoes to retain their summer sweetness, yet long enough to lose the watery quality that signals a bad sauce. When the red-orange cooked tomato pulp begins to separate from the oil, the sauce is done. Roma tomatoes are the tomatoes of choice for this and all fresh tomato sauces. Romas are a small, plum-shaped variety now seen frequently in supermarkets. Their meaty pulp has less water than round varieties; therefore when using them, you do not have to seed them, you need only cut them coarsely and cook.

12 Roma tomatoes or 6 large red ripe tomatoes

¼ cup extra-virgin olive oil, plus extra for drizzling

2–3 garlic cloves, peeled and minced

Pinch of red chile pepper flakes

5–6 large fresh basil leaves

Salt to taste

1 pound imported penne

Freshly grated Parmesan cheese

Remove the stems of the tomatoes and cut in half crosswise. If using regular round tomatoes, remove most of the seeds, using your fingers. These tomatoes tend to have excess liquid and seeds. Cut the tomatoes into quarters. Heat the extra-virgin olive oil in a large skillet over moderate heat. Add the garlic and red chile flakes. As soon as the garlic gives off its aroma and becomes opaque, add the tomatoes. Cook over high heat until the tomatoes begin to thicken. Use a wooden spoon to stir and help break up the tomato pulp. Add the basil, either whole or roughly chopped, and salt. When the sauce is cooked, remove it from the heat and put it through a food mill using the medium disk. This will remove the skins and create a completely smooth texture. Cook the pasta in abundant boiling salted water until al dente. Quickly drain and place in a serving bowl with the tomato sauce. Drizzle a little extra-virgin olive oil over the pasta and mix well with the sauce. Pass Parmesan cheese.

Sweet Tomato Sauce

SERVES 4 TO 6

Another basic sauce. The carrot and onion make it taste sweeter than the simpler Tomato-Basil Sauce (see page 128), and the celery gives it a stronger base. We like to use this sauce with stuffed pastas, in lasagne, and occasionally on a simple dish of spaghettini. The food mill is an indispensable part of any kitchen. It enables you to make fresh sauces quickly without having to peel the tomatoes first, and it gives the sauces a smooth, dense texture. Using a food processor adds air to the sauce, and, of course, you have the added task of peeling the tomatoes.

¼ cup extra-virgin olive oil
2 garlic cloves, peeled and minced
½ small onion, peeled and minced
1 small celery stalk, minced
1 carrot, peeled and minced

6 large red ripe tomatoes or 12 Roma tomatoes, coarsely chopped, or 1 28-ounce can imported Italian tomatoes, drained and coarsely chopped
2–3 fresh basil leaves
Salt and freshly ground black pepper to taste
1 pound spaghettini

Heat the extra-virgin olive oil in a skillet. Add the garlic, onion, celery, and carrot. Cook over medium heat until the onion and celery are somewhat tender, approximately 10 minutes. Add the tomatoes and continue to cook over moderate heat until the tomatoes give up juice and begin to thicken. Add the basil, salt, and pepper. When the sauce is thick enough to coat a spoon, remove it from the heat and pass it through the coarse blade of a food mill. Cook the pasta in abundant boiling salted water until al dente. Quickly drain and place in a serving bowl with the tomato sauce. Drizzle a little extra-virgin olive oil over the pasta and mix well with the sauce. Pass Parmesan cheese.

Pasta al Basilico con Noci

BASIL-FLAVORED PASTA WITH WALNUTS

*T*his unusual pasta is our version of a traditional Sardinian specialty. The basil-scented pasta adds another dimension to the dish. Its sweet fragrance mingles with the earthy taste of the nuts, the garlic-crunch of the bread crumbs, and the pungent sweetness of the tomatoes to create a light flavorful meal.

8 *tablespoons (1 stick) unsalted butter*

2 *tablespoons extra-virgin olive oil*

1 *onion, peeled and minced*

2½ *cups coarsely chopped walnuts*

Salt and freshly ground black pepper to taste

2½ *cups Coarse Seasoned Bread Crumbs (see page 46)*

12 *sun-dried tomatoes, coarsely chopped*

1 *recipe Pasta all'Erbe made with basil (see page 35), cut into fettuccine*

Melt the butter together with the extra-virgin olive oil in a medium skillet. Add the onion and cook over moderate heat until very soft and just beginning to brown at the edges. Add the walnuts to the skillet and toast lightly over moderate heat. Add the salt and pepper to taste. Add the bread crumbs and sun-dried tomatoes to the skillet and heat through.

Cook the fettuccine in abundant boiling salted water until al dente or tender, depending on which pasta-making method you use. Drain the pasta, but reserve some of the pasta cooking water. Toss the drained pasta in a shallow serving bowl with the onion-walnut-bread-crumb mixture. Add 3 to 4 tablespoons of the reserved pasta cooking water to help moisten the pasta. Serve immediately.

Dragon Sauce

*F*resh red chile peppers spice up this sauce, and ginger lends heat and fragrance. The fully ripened peppers have a satisfying rounded flavor that has a touch of sweetness to complement the fiery bite. The small bits of bright red chile look striking against the white gold of the pasta as it cooks. For another recipe from Simonetta, see page 86.

6 tablespoons extra-virgin olive oil

3 anchovies

4 medium tomatoes, peeled, seeded, and cut into strips

Small handful finely chopped Italian parsley

2 fresh red chile peppers, finely chopped, divided

½ teaspoon freshly ground black pepper

1 teaspoon ground ginger

1 garlic clove, peeled and lightly crushed

1 pound imported spaghettini

Salt

In a large sauté pan gently heat the extra-virgin olive oil and anchovies. When the anchovies blend into the oil, add the tomatoes, parsley, half the chopped red chile peppers, black pepper, ginger, and garlic clove. Cook over high heat for several minutes. Place the remaining red chile peppers in a large pot of water. Bring to a boil, add the pasta, and cook until al dente. Drain the pasta and chopped chile peppers. Remove the garlic clove from the sauce and toss sauce with the hot pasta.

Penne alla Napoletana

SERVES 4 TO 6

*I*n this dish the pasta is heated with the hot sauce and the cheese to create a rich blend. As the smoked mozzarella melts, it suffuses the pasta with its distinctive smoky flavor. This is a favorite dish of the Morra family from Naples.

1 *pound imported penne rigate*
1 *recipe Rich Fast Sauce (see page 189) or Simple Tomato-Basil Sauce (see page 128)*

¼ *pound smoked mozzarella, cut into ½-inch dice*
Freshly grated Parmesan cheese

Cook the penne rigate in abundant boiling salted water until al dente. Meanwhile, heat the tomato sauce of your choice in a large skillet. When the sauce is hot, turn off the heat, toss in the mozzarella, and lightly stir into the sauce. When the penne are cooked, drain immediately and add to the skillet containing the tomato sauce and mozzarella. Stir over high heat, allowing the sauce to penetrate the pasta and the cheese to melt. Serve immediately. Pass Parmesan cheese.

Penne alla Pizzaiola

PENNE PIZZA STYLE

Combines all the ingredients of a classic pizza. The fresh white mozzarella melts slightly when it is tossed with the hot sauce and penne.

¼ cup extra-virgin olive oil

2–3 garlic cloves, peeled and minced

1 28-ounce can imported Italian tomatoes

1 teaspoon dried oregano

Salt and freshly ground black pepper

1 pound imported penne

4–6 ounces fresh mozzarella in water, drained and roughly chopped

Freshly grated Parmesan cheese

Heat the extra-virgin olive oil in a medium-heavy skillet. Add the garlic and cook over medium heat until garlic becomes opaque and gives off its aroma. Lift the tomatoes out of their juice and crush with your fingers while adding them to the skillet. Add the oregano and cook until the tomatoes thicken into a sauce. Add salt and pepper to taste. Meanwhile, cook the pasta in abundant boiling salted water until al dente. Quickly drain and place in a shallow serving bowl. Toss the pasta with the mozzarella and the tomato sauce. Serve immediately. Pass Parmesan cheese.

Tagliatelle a Sfinciuni

SERVES 4 TO 6

This is a take on the famous Sicilian pizza called sfinciuni. Here fresh pasta is the tender foil for a savory sauce. The toasted bread crumbs serve the same function as grated cheese — to bring together the sauce and pasta — and add a final crunch.

¼ cup extra-virgin olive oil, plus 1 teaspoon

4 garlic cloves, peeled and minced

½ cup minced Italian parsley

10 anchovies

1 28-ounce can imported Italian tomatoes, drained, seeded, and pureed

Salt and freshly ground black pepper

½ cup untoasted bread crumbs (see page 46)

1 pound fresh tagliatelle or 1 recipe Pasta all'Uovo I or II, (see page 32–33), cut into tagliatelle

In a large sauté pan combine ¼ cup extra-virgin olive oil with the garlic and parsley. Sauté for 3 to 4 minutes over low heat. Add the anchovies and stir until they dissolve. Add the pureed tomatoes, season with a little salt and pepper, and cook over medium heat for 15 to 20 minutes or until the sauce thickens. In a small sauté pan combine 1 teaspoon olive oil with the bread crumbs and toast over medium heat, stirring constantly, until they turn a rich golden brown. Transfer bread crumbs to a small bowl. Cook the tagliatelle in abundant boiling salted water until tender but firm. Drain well and place in a warmed serving dish and toss with the sauce. Sprinkle a little of the toasted bread crumbs on top and serve extra bread crumbs on the side.

Penne all'Arrabiata
PENNE WITH SPICY TOMATO SAUCE

SERVES 4 TO 6

Arrabiata means "angry" and therein lies the key to the character of this sauce. At Da Lucia in Trastevere, Silvana makes the ultimate version of this popular Roman pasta. She combines the dusty spice of chile with the burning bite of raw garlic. Her final touch is to throw in a handful of raw green parsley as she tosses the pasta. Its freshness is a welcome cooling note.

¼ *cup extra-virgin olive oil*
2–3 *teaspoons red chile pepper flakes*
1 *28-ounce can imported Italian tomatoes*

3 *garlic cloves, peeled*
Salt
1 *pound imported penne*
Handful chopped Italian parsley

Heat the extra-virgin olive oil in a skillet over moderate heat. Add the chile pepper flakes. As soon as the flakes begin to add some color to the oil, lift out the tomatoes from the can and crush them with your fingers as you add them to the skillet. An alternative is to set a food mill over the skillet and puree the tomatoes directly into it. Stir the pureed tomatoes, mixing well with the oil and chile pepper flakes. Squeeze the garlic cloves through a press directly into the sauce. Add salt to taste. Cook the sauce over moderately high heat until the tomatoes begin to break down and the sauce thickens, approximately 15 minutes. Meanwhile, cook the penne in abundant boiling salted water until al dente. Quickly drain and place in a serving bowl along with tomato sauce. Add chopped parsley and mix the pasta well with the sauce.

Linguine Fini alla Dispensa
LINGUINE FINI FROM THE PANTRY

SERVES 4 TO 6

W hen you think there's nothing in the house to eat, your pantry can provide this exotic-tasting surprise.

¼ *cup extra-virgin olive oil*
1 *large onion, peeled and finely diced*
10 *large bay leaves*
1 *28-ounce can imported Italian tomatoes, seeded and pureed*
½ *teaspoon cinnamon*

½ *teaspoon ground ginger*
Pinch of nutmeg
Pinch of ground cloves
Salt and freshly ground black pepper to taste
1 *pound imported linguine fini*
Freshly grated Parmesan cheese

In a large sauté pan combine the extra-virgin olive oil, onion, and bay leaves. Cook over low heat until onion is translucent. Add the pureed tomatoes and spices. Simmer until the sauce thickens, about 15 minutes. Cook the pasta in abundant boiling salted water. Drain well and toss with the sauce. Serve with grated Parmesan cheese on the side.

Spicy Tomato and Arugola Sauce with Spaghettini

SERVES 4 TO 6

This dish is another tomato and arugola combination. In Italy arugola is often cooked as a green in soups or as a vegetable side dish. Here the arugola is added to the pasta raw when its peppery bite is at its strongest. Buy sun-dried tomato paste or make your own by puréeing oil-packed sun-dried tomatoes in the food processor. If both are unavailable, use imported tomato paste.

¼ cup extra-virgin olive oil, plus 1 tablespoon

3 garlic cloves, peeled and minced

½ teaspoon red chile pepper flakes

1 28-ounce can imported Italian tomatoes, drained, seeded, and pureed

2 tablespoons sun-dried tomato paste

Salt

1 pound imported spaghettini

½ cup pitted and quartered oil-cured black olives

2–3 bunches tender arugola, stems trimmed

Freshly grated Parmesan cheese

Gently heat ¼ cup extra-virgin olive oil, garlic, and red chile pepper in a large sauté pan. When the garlic releases its aroma, add the pureed tomatoes, sun-dried tomato paste, and salt to taste. Cook over medium-low heat until the sauce thickens, about 20 minutes. Cook the spaghettini in abundant boiling salted water. Place the olives and arugola in a serving bowl. When the pasta is al dente, drain well, and transfer to a serving bowl with 1 tablespoon extra-virgin olive oil. Toss quickly, add the sauce, and toss again. Serve with Parmesan cheese on the side.

PASTA DEL GIARDINO
138

Fusilli alla Siracusana
FUSILLI SYRACUSE STYLE

SERVES 4 TO 6

A famous sauce from Syracuse in Sicily. A light hand is needed to maintain its freshness and immediacy; do not overcook. Use the eggplant unpeeled — the skin helps hold the flesh together, all the while adding its beautiful deep purple gloss.

1 *medium eggplant*
Salt
¼ *cup extra-virgin olive oil, plus 1 tablespoon*
2 *garlic cloves, peeled and lightly crushed*
4 *large red ripe tomatoes, peeled, seeded, and chopped*
2 *red or yellow peppers, roasted, peeled, and cut into strips*

3 *anchovies, chopped to a paste*
½ *cup pitted and quartered oil-cured black olives*
1 *heaping tablespoon capers*
Small bunch fresh basil, leaves coarsely chopped, divided
Freshly ground black pepper
1 *pound imported fusilli*
Freshly grated Pecorino Romano cheese

Trim the eggplant and cut into ½ -inch dice. Sprinkle with salt and set aside in a colander to drain for about 1 hour. Dry the eggplant well. In a large sauté pan brown the garlic cloves in ¼ cup extra-virgin olive oil. Discard the garlic. To the flavored oil add the diced eggplant, chopped tomatoes, peppers, anchovies, olives, capers, and half the basil. Cover and simmer for 15 to 20 minutes. Taste for salt; it may not require any. Add pepper to taste. Cook the pasta in abundant boiling salted water until al dente. Drain well and toss with 1 tablespoon olive oil. Add the sauce, toss, and sprinkle with the remaining basil. Pass Pecorino Romano cheese.

Spaghetti alla Fantasia

SERVES 4 TO 6

*E*very once in a while a new vegetable comes along whose taste equals its beauty. The orange bell pepper is just such a one. A rich, deep golden orange, its taste is perhaps the sweetest of all the ripe peppers. In this dish its sweet taste is reinforced by the onion and basil; the salty tang of the Gorgonzola sets it all in relief.

¼ cup extra-virgin olive oil
1 onion, peeled and minced
4 orange bell peppers, stems removed, seeded, and cut into thin lengthwise slices
3–4 fresh basil leaves, cut into julienne

½ pound dolce latte Gorgonzola
Salt and freshly ground black pepper to taste
1 pound imported spaghetti
Freshly grated Parmesan cheese

Heat the extra-virgin olive oil in a skillet. Add the onion and pepper slices. Cook over low heat until the onion and peppers are tender and just beginning to brown at the edges. Add the basil, salt, and black pepper toward the end of the cooking time. Cook the spaghetti in abundant boiling salted water until al dente. Drain well and place in shallow serving bowl. Crumble the Gorgonzola over the hot spaghetti and toss gently so the cheese starts to melt. Add the onion-pepper mixture and toss again. Pass Parmesan cheese.

Spaghettini alla Bellini

*A*nother regional sauce from Sicily, named after the famous opera composer Vincenzo Bellini. This pasta looks beautiful with its small fans of eggplant covering each serving and its snowy sprinkling of cheese. It is cooked more traditionally with one large eggplant cut into a fan shape, deep fried, and placed on top of a large serving bowl filled with pasta. In Palermo, you can go to the marketplace and buy a whole fried eggplant from one of the vendors, take it home, and use it in your pasta dish. Dry ricotta salata is salted ricotta that is aged long enough to have a hard consistency suitable for grating.

6 *small Japanese eggplants*
Salt
¼ *cup extra-virgin olive oil*
2 *garlic cloves, peeled and minced*
1 *28-ounce can imported Italian tomatoes*
1 *bunch fresh basil, leaves coarsely chopped, divided*

Freshly ground black pepper to taste
Olive oil for frying
1 *pound imported spaghettini*
¼ *pound dry ricotta salata, grated*

Slice the eggplants into fans by cutting them lengthwise toward the stem ends. Make 3 or 4 slices in each, but keep the stem end intact. Gently spread out the slices to form a fan. Arrange on paper towels, sprinkle with salt, and set aside to drain for about 1 hour. Meanwhile, in a large sauté pan combine the extra-virgin olive oil and garlic. Sauté over low heat for 2 to 3 minutes. Pass the tomatoes and their juices through a food mill directly into the pan. Add half the chopped basil, and the pepper, and cook over medium heat until the sauce thickens, about 15 minutes. Pat the eggplant dry. Pour enough olive oil in a large skillet to come up ⅜ inch. When oil is very hot but not smoking, fry the eggplants a few at a time without crowding the pan, until crisp and golden. Drain on paper towels. Sprinkle with salt and keep warm. Cook the spaghettini in abundant boiling salted water until al dente. Drain well and toss with the sauce and the rest of the chopped basil. Arrange the eggplant fans over the top and sprinkle with the grated ricotta salata.

Fusilli con Rapini e Pomodoro

Rapini, or broccoli rabe, is a tasty vegetable with the unusual bitter edge that Italians find so pleasing. It originally grew wild and was collected from the fields to be cooked as a green. Whole-wheat fusilli add their earthy flavor to this dish.

2–3 *garlic cloves, finely chopped*

½ *teaspoon red chile pepper flakes*

3 *tablespoons extra-virgin olive oil*

1½ *pounds tomatoes, peeled, seeded, and chopped*

½ *bunch fresh basil, leaves coarsely chopped*

2 *sprigs fresh oregano, leaves finely chopped*

Salt and freshly ground black pepper to taste

1 *bunch rapini, stems trimmed and yellow leaves discarded*

1 *pound imported whole-wheat fusilli*

Freshly grated Pecorino Romano cheese

Combine the garlic, red chile pepper, and extra-virgin olive oil in a sauté pan. Cook for several minutes until garlic begins to color slightly. Add the tomatoes, basil, oregano, salt, and pepper. Raise the heat to medium and cook uncovered for about 10 minutes. Meanwhile, cook the rapini in abundant boiling salted water until tender. Lift rapini out of the water, reserving the cooking liquid in the pot. Drain the rapini and coarsely chop. Add to the tomato sauce and cook for an additional 5 minutes. Bring the reserved water to a boil, add the fusilli, and cook until al dente. Drain well and combine with the sauce. Sprinkle with Pecorino Romano cheese and serve immediately.

Maccheroni con Peperoni

MACARONI WITH YELLOW PEPPERS

SERVES 4 TO 6

This was inspired by a recipe from the Abruzzi. It is important to brown the garlic really well to develop the rich taste, but make sure it doesn't burn, as the flavor becomes too bitter. Mint leaves are an untraditional touch, lending an unexpectedly fresh accent to the finished dish. Yellow peppers are incredibly sweet. Buy those with a developed gold color, but make sure they're not soft or withered. The peppers should be firm and heavy, especially when they are to be roasted. A fleshier pepper stays crisp after peeling.

¼ cup extra-virgin olive oil

3 garlic cloves, peeled and lightly crushed

2 slices pancetta, cut ¼ inch thick, chopped

½ teaspoon crushed dried red chile pepper

4 large yellow bell peppers, roasted, peeled, seeded, and cut into strips

1 28-ounce can imported Italian tomatoes, drained, seeded, and coarsely chopped

Salt and freshly ground black pepper

1 pound imported tubetti

Small handful fresh mint leaves, coarsely chopped

Freshly grated Pecorino Romano cheese

Combine the extra-virgin olive oil, garlic, pancetta, and red chile pepper in a large sauté pan. Over low heat cook until the garlic is golden and the pancetta has rendered some of its fat. Add the yellow peppers to the pan.

Raise the heat to medium, and sauté the peppers in the flavored oil for a few minutes. Add the tomatoes, salt, and pepper, and cook until juices thicken. Meanwhile, cook the pasta in abundant boiling salted water. When al dente, drain well, place in a serving dish, and toss with the sauce. Sprinkle with chopped mint and some of the Pecorino Romano cheese. Toss again and serve with additional grated cheese on the side.

Spaghetti con Fagiolini
SPAGHETTI WITH GREEN BEANS

SERVES 4 TO 6

Try to find the most thin, tender yet crisp beans. The broad, flat Romano beans are also delicious in this dish. Braising the beans instead of blanching them adds extra flavor.

½ *pound tender green or yellow beans, or a mixture*

2–3 *garlic cloves, peeled and minced*

¼ *cup extra-virgin olive oil*

10 *fresh basil leaves*

4 *sun-dried tomatoes, sliced thinly*

Salt and freshly ground black pepper to taste

1 *pound imported spaghetti*

Freshly grated Parmesan cheese

Wash the beans and remove any strings. Cook the garlic in the extra-virgin olive oil over low heat until the garlic becomes opaque and gives off its characteristic aroma. Add the beans, basil, sun-dried tomatoes, salt, and pepper, and stir ingredients to coat with garlic and oil. Cook over medium heat until the beans are tender, adding ¼ cup water, if necessary. Cook the pasta in abundant boiling salted water until al dente. Quickly drain and place in a shallow serving bowl. Add beans. Gently toss the pasta and serve immediately. Pass Parmesan cheese.

Fettuccine con Verdura alla Griglia
GRILLED VEGGIE PASTA

SERVES 4 TO 6

A dish suffused with the strong, deep flavor of the grill, a good pasta to prepare in advance. The vegetables can be grilled earlier in the day and mixed with the herbs and sun-dried tomatoes, then left to marinate until you are ready to cook the pasta and serve. Other vegetables that take well to this sauce include radicchio, fennel, and zucchini, to name just a few. Very adaptable to each passing season.

5 baby artichokes

Cut lemon

2 heads Belgian endive

2 leeks

½ cup extra-virgin olive oil, plus additional to taste

Juice of 1 lemon

Handful of mixed fresh herbs (basil, oregano, parsley, thyme)

1 pound fresh fettuccine or 1 recipe Pasta all'Uovo I or II (see pages 32–33), cut into fettuccine

6 sun-dried tomatoes, cut into thin strips

¼ onion, peeled and minced

2 garlic cloves, peeled and minced, divided

Salt and freshly ground black pepper to taste

Trim the artichokes and cut in half lengthwise. Rub with the cut lemon. Slice the Belgian endive in half lengthwise; trim the root ends. Trim away the tough leaves of the leeks and trim the root ends. To clean, make deep vertical incisions halfway up from the root through the leaves and rinse the leeks well under cold running water. Cut in half lengthwise and drain well.

Make a marinade by combining ½ cup extra-virgin olive oil with the lemon juice and herbs in a glass or enamel bowl. Add the onion, 1 clove minced garlic, artichokes, endive, and leeks to the marinade and let sit at room temperature for at least 2 hours, preferably more. Just before grilling, lift the vegetables out of the marinade and let drain. Reserve marinade.

Using a charcoal grill or a cast-iron ridged griddle, grill the vegetables on both sides, turning once, until they are tender but not burned or overcooked. Remove the vegetables from the grill, and as they cool cut them into a julienne.

Cook the fresh fettuccine in abundant boiling salted water until al dente. Drain well and place in shallow pasta serving bowl. Add the grilled vegetables, the sun-dried tomatoes, 1 clove minced garlic, the reserved marinade, salt, pepper, and extra-virgin olive oil to taste, and toss.

Zucchini Sauce Capri Style

Here the zucchini is cooked until it becomes like a coarse puree, not tender-crisp, an unusual way to cook zucchini for pasta. We ate this dish on the island of Capri in a trattoria set in the middle of a grove of lemon trees. On that warm evening, everyone sat outside at tables under the stars. The trattoria's specialties were pasta with zucchini sauce and rabbit stew, washed down with island wine.

¼ cup extra-virgin olive oil

1 large onion, peeled and finely diced

1 large garlic clove, peeled and minced

1½ pounds tender zucchini, trimmed and cut into small dice

2 large tomatoes, peeled, seeded, and coarsely chopped

10 sprigs Italian parsley, leaves finely chopped

1 cup warm water or chicken broth

Salt

1 pound imported spaghettini

5 fresh basil leaves, torn

Freshly grated Parmesan cheese

Combine the extra-virgin olive oil, onion, and garlic in a sauté pan. Cook over low heat until the onion softens. Add the zucchini, tomatoes, parsley, and water or broth. Season with salt. Cover and cook at a gentle simmer until the zucchini becomes very soft like a coarse puree, about 20 minutes. Cook the pasta in abundant boiling salted water until al dente. Drain well and toss with the sauce. Taste for salt. Sprinkle with basil and serve with Parmesan cheese on the side.

Fusilli con Zucchini e Basilico

The sweet flavors of zucchini and basil combine beautifully with butter to create a simple but delicious sauce for fusilli. Select small, firm zucchini. Larger ones have tough, developed seeds and are watery and less delicate in flavor.

2 small, firm zucchini

1 small, firm yellow zucchini, or crookneck squash

3 tablespoons unsalted butter

1 tablespoon extra-virgin olive oil

4–5 garlic cloves, peeled and chopped

6 fresh basil leaves, chopped

Salt and freshly ground black pepper

1 pound imported fusilli

Freshly grated Parmesan cheese

Cut the green and yellow zucchini into julienne by slicing each squash lengthwise into four long strips. Lay the strips one on top of the other and cut them horizontally into very thin strips, or julienne. Set aside. Heat the butter and extra-virgin olive oil together in a medium skillet. When the butter is melted and the foam begins to subside, add the chopped garlic to the skillet and cook over medium heat until garlic becomes opaque. Add the zucchini and basil. Cook over medium-high heat until the zucchini softens and some pieces are golden brown, approximately 7 minutes. Do not overcook! Add salt and pepper to taste. Cook the pasta in abundant boiling salted water until al dente. Quickly drain and place in a shallow serving bowl with the zucchini and all the cooking juices. Gently toss the pasta and serve immediately. Pass Parmesan cheese.

Maccheroni alla Fattoria
FARM-STYLE MACARONI

SERVES 4 TO 6

*A*lla fattoria refers to the farmhouse character of this sauce — vegetables from the fields, a ham curing in the attic, a little local wine, combined with good chunky pasta — rough and elegant simultaneously. Light cooking keeps the sauce fresh and maintains the integrity of the textures and flavors. It's fun to imagine a farmer's wife, mixing odds and ends of dried pasta. Use your imagination when combining pasta shapes, and select those that have the same cooking times.

¼ cup extra-virgin olive oil

2 tablespoons unsalted butter

1 large onion, finely diced

2 medium zucchini, trimmed and diced

¼ pound best-quality cooked ham, trimmed and diced

2 medium potatoes, peeled, diced, and cooked in boiling salted water until tender but very firm

Salt and freshly ground black pepper

½ cup dry white wine

1 pound imported mixed short pasta, such as elbows, fusilli, or penne

Small handful chopped Italian parsley

Freshly grated Parmesan cheese

Combine the extra-virgin olive oil and butter in a sauté pan. Add the onion and sauté until translucent. Add the zucchini, ham, and potatoes, and season with salt and pepper. Sauté for several minutes or until the zucchini is tender but crisp and the ham is lightly colored. Add the wine. Cover and simmer for about 5 minutes. Cook the pasta in abundant boiling salted water. Drain when al dente. Toss with the sauce and the parsley, and sprinkle with a little Parmesan cheese. Serve immediately.

Orecchiette con Cime di Rapa
LITTLE EARS WITH RAPINI

SERVES 4 TO 6

Rapini, also known as broccoli rabe, is a robust green vegetable with a bitter edge to it. Here it is cooked with the pasta and then tossed with a tangy mixture of olive oil, garlic, red chile peppers, and anchovies. Anchovies work well in fast pasta sauces, adding a tremendous depth of flavor — not fishy as so many people fear.

½ *cup extra-virgin olive oil*	*Salt*
4 *garlic cloves, peeled and minced*	1 *pound imported orecchiette*
2 *dried red chile peppers, crushed*	2 *bunches rapini, tough stems trimmed, leaves and tender stems coarsely chopped*
6 *anchovies*	

Combine the extra-virgin olive oil, garlic, and red chile peppers in a small sauté pan. Cook over low heat briefly. Add the anchovies and stir until they dissolve. Meanwhile, bring an abundant amount of water to a boil. Add salt, stir, and add the pasta. When the water returns to a boil, add the rapini and cook until the pasta is tender. Drain well. In a warmed serving dish, combine the pasta, rapini, and flavored oil. Toss well and correct the seasonings. Serve immediately.

Farfalle Medie con Piselli e Prosciutto
BOW TIES WITH PEAS

SERVES 4 TO 6

*C*ooking the onions until just lightly browned and deglazing the pan produce a savory light sauce in this simple, comforting dish.

¼ *cup extra-virgin olive oil*

½ *medium onion, peeled and finely diced*

12 *ounces fresh shelled peas*

6 *ounces thickly sliced prosciutto, cut into thin strips*

10 *fresh basil leaves*

1 *pound imported farfalle medie (bow ties)*

1 *tablespoon soft unsalted butter*

Freshly grated Parmesan cheese

Heat the extra-virgin olive oil in a small skillet. Add the onion and cook over medium heat until onion is wilted and beginning to brown at the edges. Add the prosciutto and basil to the onion and sauté just until the prosciutto changes color. Add 2 cups water to the onion-prosciutto mixture to deglaze the pan of the caramelized onion bits. Add the peas, salt, and pepper to taste and bring the peas to a simmer in the pan. Cover and gently cook the peas until they are completely tender. They will lose their bright green color. Meanwhile, cook the pasta in abundant boiling salted water. When the pasta is al dente, quickly drain and place in a shallow serving bowl. Toss the pasta with butter. Add the pea mixture. Gently toss the pasta and sprinkle a small handful of Parmesan cheese on top as a garnish. Serve immediately. Pass Parmesan cheese.

Fettuccine with Rapini and Radicchio

The mellow, egg-rich homemade fettuccine combines with the sweet slowly cooked onion to tame the slightly bitter edge of the rapini and radicchio.

1 bunch rapini, thick stems removed, leaves and tender stems coarsely cut

¼ cup extra-virgin olive oil

½ medium onion, peeled and thinly sliced

3 garlic cloves, peeled and thinly sliced

1 head radicchio, core removed, shredded

Salt and freshly ground black pepper to taste

1 pound homemade fettuccine or 1 recipe Pasta all'Uovo I or II (see pages 32–33), cut into fettuccine

Bring a large pot of water to a boil. Add the rapini and quickly bring back to the boil. Cook rapini for only 1 to 2 minutes, then quickly drain. This will remove any excess bitterness from the vegetable. Heat the extra-virgin olive oil in a large skillet. Add the onion and cook slowly over medium heat, stirring frequently, until the onion is wilted and translucent. Add the garlic and cook until it gives off its characteristic aroma. Add the radicchio and rapini, and sauté over medium heat, stirring, until the vegetables are tender. Add salt and pepper. Cook the pasta in abundant boiling salted water until al dente. Quickly drain and transfer to a warmed serving bowl. Add the hot vegetable sauce, quickly toss, and serve immediately.

Tagliolini con Rughetta
THIN HOMEMADE PASTA WITH ARUGOLA
SERVES 4 TO 6

Cooked arugola has a light delicacy that stronger greens lack. The peppery quality it has in its raw state softens. We can imagine this pasta dish being served in a fine Roman restaurant, with the mozzarella, freshly arrived from Naples, still moist from its milky bath. To cut tagliolini, keep the fresh pasta sheets a little thick so that when you use the fine cutting roller, the pasta ends up like square spaghetti.

2 tablespoons unsalted butter

¼ cup extra-virgin olive oil

½ medium onion, peeled and chopped

4 bunches arugola, washed and stems discarded

1 pound fresh tagliolini or 1 recipe Pasta all'Uovo I or II (page 32–33), cut into tagliolini

8 ounces mozzarella packed in water, diced

Salt and freshly ground black pepper to taste

Freshly grated Parmesan cheese

Melt the butter with the extra-virgin olive oil in a small skillet. Add the onion and cook slowly over medium heat until it is soft and translucent. Add the arugola and stir occasionally until it is wilted and tender, approximately 5 minutes. Add salt and pepper. Start cooking the pasta in abundant boiling salted water. While the pasta is cooking, put the diced mozzarella into a shallow serving bowl. When the pasta is al dente, quickly drain and place in the shallow serving bowl. Toss the hot pasta with the mozzarella. Immediately add the onion-arugola mixture and gently stir into the pasta. Serve immediately. Pass Parmesan cheese.

Spaghetti Integrale con Cime di Rapa

WHOLE-WHEAT SPAGHETTI WITH RAPINI

SERVES 4 TO 6

*T*his is a rustic combination if ever there was one, with the strong flavor of bitter greens and the warm toasty flavor of whole-wheat pasta. The roasted garlic has a gutsy nutty taste that is very different from the peppery bite of the raw cloves.

- 2 *bunches rapini, washed*
- ½ *cup extra-virgin olive oil*
- 1 *onion, peeled and thinly sliced*
- 2 *slices pancetta, coarsely chopped*
- 1 *garlic clove, peeled and minced*

Pinch of red chile pepper flakes

- 6–8 *garlic cloves, peeled and left whole*

Salt to taste

- 1 *pound imported whole-wheat spaghetti*

Freshly grated Parmesan cheese

Remove any coarse rapini stems. Cut the rapini crosswise into coarse, thick strips. Heat the extra-virgin olive oil in a medium skillet. Add the onion. Cook over medium heat for 2 to 3 minutes. Add the pancetta and cook until it begins to give off its fat. Add the minced garlic, rapini, red chile flakes, and salt. Meanwhile, place the whole garlic cloves in a pie tin. Roast the garlic in a preheated 450° oven or place under the broiler until the cloves turn a deep golden brown in spots and just soften. Add the roasted garlic to the skillet with the rapini mixture. Cook just until the rapini is tender. Cook the pasta in abundant boiling salted water until al dente. Quickly drain and transfer to a shallow serving bowl. Add the rapini mixture and toss. Pass Parmesan cheese.

Rigatoni alla Cinese

RIGATONI CHINESE STYLE

SERVES 4 TO 6

We call this dish Chinese Style because it is cooked quickly so that it still has a fresh, crunchy bite.

1½ *pounds tender broccoli*
 1 *pound imported rigatoni*
 ½ *cup extra-virgin olive oil*
 3 *garlic cloves, peeled and thinly sliced*

Salt
Freshly grated Parmesan cheese

Trim the broccoli ends and peel the stalks. Quarter the broccoli lengthwise and cut into pieces about 2 inches long. Cook the pasta in abundant boiling salted water. About 4 to 5 minutes before the pasta is cooked, add the broccoli. Drain when the pasta and broccoli are both cooked al dente. Place in a serving dish, drizzle with the extra-virgin olive oil, sprinkle with the garlic, season with the salt, and toss gently. Serve with grated cheese on the side.

Pasta con Indivia

PASTA WITH BELGIAN ENDIVE

SERVES 4 TO 6

At first glance this arresting combination of slightly bitter endive and sweet onion, seems totally untraditional. However, Belgian endive is a logical substitute for the long, tapered radicchio di Treviso, so rarely seen in the United States.

3 *Belgian endive heads*
¼ *cup extra-virgin olive oil*
1 *medium onion, peeled and sliced thin*
2 *slices pancetta, coarsely chopped*
12 *fresh basil leaves*
Salt and freshly ground black pepper to taste
½ *cup dry white wine*

½ *cup chicken broth*
1 *pound homemade fettuccine or whole-wheat fettuccine, or 1 recipe Pasta all'Uovo I or II (see pages 32–33), or 1 recipe Pasta Integrale (see page 33), cut into fettuccine*
Freshly grated Parmesan cheese

Trim the endive root ends to remove any blemishes. Cut each head in half lengthwise and wash carefully. Lay on paper or cloth towels to dry. Cut the endive halves lengthwise into julienne. Set aside. Heat the extra-virgin olive oil in a medium skillet. Add the onion. Cook over medium heat for 2 to 3 minutes. Add the pancetta and cook until it begins to give off its fat. Add the endive, basil, salt, and pepper. Cook the endive just until it wilts. Deglaze the pan with the wine and chicken broth. Set aside. Cook the pasta in abundant boiling salted water until al dente. Quickly drain and place in a shallow serving bowl. Toss the pasta with 1 to 2 tablespoons of extra-virgin olive oil. Add the endive mixture and toss. Pass Parmesan cheese.

Fettuccine al Finocchio
HOMEMADE PASTA WITH FENNEL
SERVES 4 TO 6

Fennel is an extraordinary vegetable. Raw, it has a pronounced licorice flavor with a texture that is crisper and juicier than celery. When cooked, it becomes creamy sweet. In this dish that sweetness is balanced by the acidity of the tomatoes. The fennel turns glossy, with the absorbed juices of the pancetta creating a succulent, rich plate of pasta.

2 *bulbs fennel*

1 *medium onion, peeled and thinly sliced*

¼ *cup extra-virgin olive oil*

6 *ounces pancetta, coarsely chopped*

8 *Roma tomatoes, peeled, seeded, and roughly chopped*

10–15 *fresh basil leaves*

Salt and freshly ground black pepper to taste

1 *pound homemade fettuccine, or 1 recipe Pasta all'Uovo I or II (page 32–33), cut into fettuccine*

Freshly grated Parmesan cheese

Trim the fibrous stems from the fennel bulbs. If the outer layers are extremely tough, discard them. Cut the fennel into thin crosswise slices. Cook the onion and fennel together in the extra-virgin olive oil. When they are halfway cooked, add the tomatoes and basil to the pan and continue cooking until the onions and fennel are wilted and translucent. Cook the pancetta in a separate pan until it renders its fat but is not crispy. Add the cooked pancetta and all of its fat to the onion-fennel mixture. Add salt and pepper to taste and mix thoroughly. Cook the pasta in abundant boiling salted water until al dente. Quickly drain and place in a shallow serving bowl. Add the fennel mixture. Gently toss the pasta and serve immediately. Pass Parmesan cheese.

Spaghetti con Broccoli

A standard dish in every southern Italian cook's repertoire, in this version the broccoli is cooked until it completely falls apart and becomes a coarse puree. The nutrients are not lost through this long cooking process because the water becomes an integral part of the sauce. The taste of browned garlic is an important feature. Italians find ways of adding deep flavor to the simplest, most economical of ingredients.

2 pounds broccoli	Salt
¼ cup extra-virgin olive oil	1 pound imported spaghetti
6–10 garlic cloves, peeled	Freshly grated Parmesan cheese
1–2 red chiles or ½ teaspoon red chile pepper flakes	

Trim off the hard dry ends of the broccoli stalks. Remove the peel from tough stalks with a vegetable peeler or sharp paring knife. Coarsely chop the broccoli. Wash and set aside. Heat the extra-virgin olive oil in a large skillet or saucepan. Add the garlic cloves and cook over medium heat until they are golden brown. Add the hot chiles, or red chile pepper flakes, and chopped broccoli. Sauté the broccoli for 1 to 2 minutes, stirring often. Add water to cover and salt to taste. Cover the pan and cook until the broccoli is very soft, adding extra water if necessary. When properly cooked, the mixture should be like a rough puree. If necessary, remove the cover and cook the broccoli over high heat to allow the juices to thicken. As the mixture cooks, stir frequently to break up the garlic cloves and broccoli flowerets. Cook the spaghetti in abundant boiling salted water until al dente. Quickly drain and place in a serving bowl with the broccoli puree. Mix the spaghetti well with the broccoli. Pass Parmesan cheese.

Rotelle al Cavolfiore Saporito
CARTWHEELS WITH SAVORY
CAULIFLOWER SAUCE

SERVES 4 TO 6

*I*nspired by a Sicilian vegetable dish. The onion, anchovies, and olives imbue this sauce with tremendous flavor. Grated caciocavallo or provolone cheese, tangy and moist, is the topping. Start your meal with bruschetta topped with chopped tomato, and end with a salad composed of arugola and a few crisp slivers of sweet vegetables.

1 *cauliflower, white and unblemished*

Salt

6 *tablespoons extra-virgin olive oil*

1 *large onion, peeled and cut into medium dice*

3 *anchovies*

16 *oil-cured black olives, pitted and coarsely chopped*

Handful Italian parsley, chopped

1 *pound imported rotelle*

Freshly ground black pepper to taste

¼ *pound grated imported provolone or caciocavallo cheese*

Remove the leaves from the cauliflower and trim the stalk. Cut the cauliflower into quarters. Bring a large pot of water to the boil. Add salt. Cook the cauliflower at a boil until tender-crisp. Drain and coarsely chop. Meanwhile, in a large sauté pan combine the extra-virgin olive oil, onion, and anchovies. Cook over low heat until the onion is tender. Add the cauliflower, black olives, and chopped parsley. Season with a little salt and cook over low heat for a few minutes to let flavors develop. Cook the pasta in abundant salted boiling water. When al dente, drain, reserving a few tablespoons of the pasta cooking water. Combine the sauce, pasta, cooking water, and pepper. Mix quickly. Sprinkle a little grated cheese on top and serve. Put remaining cheese in a small bowl and pass at the table.

Fettuccine con Asparagi
FETTUCCINE WITH ASPARAGUS

SERVES 4 TO 6

*C*ook this dish in the spring when asparagus is at its most plentiful. The thicker stalks remain al dente and add a toothsome quality.

1 *pound asparagus, medium to thick stalks*

Salt

¼ *cup extra-virgin olive oil*

3 *garlic cloves, peeled and minced*

16 *fresh basil leaves*

5 *ounces thick-cut prosciutto, cut into thin strips*

1 *pound fresh fettuccine or 1 recipe Pasta all'Uovo I or II (page 32–33), cut into fettuccine*

Freshly grated Parmesan cheese

Trim the asparagus spears so that none of the hard, fibrous bottoms remain. Bring an abundant amount of water to boil in a large pot. Add a small handful of salt. Blanch the asparagus in the boiling water just until they begin to bend. They should be cooked like pasta — al dente, or just tender to the bite with a slight crispness. Quickly drain the asparagus and place in a bowl of cold water and ice to stop the cooking process. As soon as the asparagus are cool to the touch lift the spears from the water and place on paper towels to drain. When the asparagus are dry, slice crosswise into ½-inch pieces. Set aside.

Heat the extra-virgin olive oil in a medium skillet. Add the garlic, asparagus, basil, and prosciutto. Cook lightly just until the garlic become opaque and the prosciutto turns color. Set aside. Cook the pasta in abundant boiling salted water until al dente. Quickly drain and place in a shallow serving bowl. Add the asparagus mixture. Gently toss the pasta, adding a little pasta water to moisten the dish, and serve immediately. Pass Parmesan cheese.

Farfalle Medie ai Funghi
BOW TIES WITH MUSHROOMS

S E R V E S 4 T O 6

We had this dish for lunch at Coco Lezzone, one of our favorite hangouts in Florence. It is important to cook the mushrooms hot and fast, adding salt after they're cooked. Adding the salt while they are cooking draws out their liquid, leaving them soft and flabby. The mushrooms should have a light brown crust and still have a bit of resistance. The literal translation of farfalle is "butterflies," a fanciful image that enhances the enjoyment of this fun flat shape. Farfalle are best used with simple vegetables and pasta dishes with no heavy sauce.

1 *ounce dried porcini mushrooms*

2 *pounds fresh mushrooms*

½ *stick unsalted butter*

2 *tablespoons extra-virgin olive oil*

Handful chopped Italian parsley

1 *bunch fresh basil leaves, chopped*

1 *small sprig fresh rosemary, leaves only, finely minced*

4 *garlic cloves, peeled and minced*

Salt and freshly ground black pepper to taste

1 *pound imported farfalle medie*

Freshly grated Parmesan cheese

Soak the porcini mushrooms in a small bowl of warm water for at least 20 minutes. Before using, carefully drain the porcini and wash carefully, making sure that no sand clings to the mushrooms. Cut off any remaining hard pieces. Using a damp kitchen towel, carefully wipe any dirt off the fresh mushrooms. Do not soak them in water! Trim fresh mushroom stems and slice lengthwise into pieces approximately ¼ inch thick. Melt the butter and extra-virgin olive oil together in a large sauté pan. Fry porcini and fresh mushrooms together over high heat with the herbs and garlic until the mushrooms are tender. Add salt and pepper at the end of the cooking time. Cook the pasta in abundant boiling salted water until al dente. Drain well and place the pasta in a shallow serving bowl. Add the mushrooms and a drizzle of very fine extra-virgin olive oil. Mix and serve immediately. Pass Parmesan cheese.

Gnocchi ai Carciofi
GNOCCHI WITH ARTICHOKES

SERVES 4 TO 6

The name gnocchi, in addition to referring to fresh dumplings (see pages 242–253), also refers to a shell-like dried pasta shape. This shape is great with a sauce like this one, when the vegetables are cut small, because the cuplike opening traps the savory bits.

2 lemons, cut in half

4 large, firm, unblemished artichokes

¼ cup extra-virgin olive oil

½ onion, diced fine

2 slices pancetta, coarsely chopped

6 garlic cloves, peeled and minced

½ cup dry white wine or water

Salt and freshly ground black pepper to taste

1 pound imported gnocchi

Freshly grated Parmesan cheese

Extra-virgin olive oil for drizzling

Fill a medium bowl with cold water and squeeze the lemons into it. Add the lemon halves to the water. Set aside. Holding the artichokes with the stems pointing away from you, break off the leaves row by row and discard them. Continue to remove leaves, turning each artichoke, as you go along, until only the very tender yellow leaves are left. With a sharp knife, trim the stem, leaving approximately ½ inch. Pare the tough outer layer of the stem and the bottom of the artichoke until the dark green color is gone and only white or yellow remains. Cut off the top cone so that the leaf portion that remains is yellow. Cut artichokes in half lengthwise. Using a melon baller or grapefruit spoon, carefully remove the choke and any sharp purple leaves. Cut the cleaned and trimmed artichokes into thin slices, and quickly place in the lemon water to prevent discoloration.

Heat the extra-virgin olive oil in a large, heavy skillet. Add the onion and cook over low heat until it begins to soften. Add the pancetta and cook over medium heat until it begins to give off its fat. Add the garlic. Drain the artichoke slices thoroughly of all water and add to the skillet. Continue to cook until the artichokes are tender and some pieces are golden brown. Deglaze the pan with the white wine or water, stirring to incorporate all the bits that stick to the bottom of the pan. Add salt and pepper. Remove from heat. Cook the pasta in abundant boiling salted water until al dente. Quickly drain and place in a shallow serving bowl. Toss the pasta with 1 to 2 tablespoons of extra-virgin olive oil. Add the artichoke mixture and toss again. Pass Parmesan cheese.

PASTA DEL MARE

Pasta from the Sea

*I*taly is synonymous with the sea. It is impossible to travel in any direction for very long without eventually spotting a dazzling stretch of coastline and be tantalized by the prospect of a fish dinner in a seaside trattoria. To enter a fish market in Italy is to enter a strange new world with all varieties of shelled creatures and gleaming fish, from shades of silver, pale green, and pink to blue-black and iridescent. It was natural that combinations of pasta and seafood evolved; the pasta absorbing the briny juices; the intriguing interplay of textures; and the beauty of the finished dish — the tiny gray clams or the black and coral mussels set against the golden strands of pasta.

These dishes evoke the Mediterranean — a simple dock with fishing boats painted aqua, red, yellow, and sea green, chipped and peeling from exposure to the salt water and strong sun, rusting anchors, and masses of fishing nets like careless heaps of delicate lace. In Italy little time is lost between the fisherman's return to shore and the catch that is served up in homes or restaurants, grilled, fried, in soups, and in pasta. It is this freshness that allows for simplicity of preparation.

In American markets we are able to get good-quality clams, sweet crab, silver-skinned sardines, fresh tuna, and swordfish, and there's enough variety in our choices to reproduce the spirit of Italian seafood pasta. Look for the best seafood you can find — the smallest clams, freshly cooked crab, delicate scallops. Frozen fish will never be a substitute for the fresh, although frozen shrimp and squid may sometimes be your only options. The most important thing to remember is that fresh seafood of all kinds requires careful cooking. Scallops should be as smooth as glass and as tender as the cooked white of egg. Tuna should be barely pink at the center to retain its moist texture. Clams and mussels should be cooked just until they open, and then they should be removed immediately from the heat.

PASTA DEL MARE

Spaghetti al Tonno Fresco
SPAGHETTI WITH FRESH TUNA

SERVES 4 TO 6

*T*raditional flavors of the southern Italian coastal areas are featured in this dish. We use a variation on the toasted bread crumbs typical of the south. The bread is coarsely chopped and toasted with garlic, creating a crunchy, garlicky topping.

- ¼ *cup extra-virgin olive oil*
- 1 *pound fresh tuna, cut into 1-inch pieces*
- 6 *anchovy fillets, roughly chopped*
- 10–15 *Kalamata olives, pitted and roughly chopped*
- 1 *tablespoon capers*
- ¼ *cup coarsely chopped Italian parsley*
- 1 *lemon*
- 1 *recipe Coarse Seasoned Bread Crumbs (recipe follows)*
- *Salt and freshly ground black pepper to taste*
- 1 *pound imported spaghetti*

Heat the extra-virgin olive oil in a skillet over medium heat. Add the tuna pieces, anchovies, olives, capers, and parsley. Gently sauté until the tuna is just cooked. Remove from the heat and squeeze the lemon over the tuna mixture. Cover and set aside to keep warm. Cook pasta in abundant boiling salted water until al dente. Quickly drain and place in a shallow serving bowl. Lightly toss the tuna mixture into the pasta. Sprinkle with the Toasted Bread Crumbs and serve quickly.

COARSE SEASONED BREAD CRUMBS

3 *garlic cloves, peeled and finely chopped*

3 *tablespoons extra-virgin olive oil*

2 *thick slices good-quality fresh Italian or French bread*

Sauté the garlic in the extra-virgin olive oil until the garlic becomes opaque and gives off its aroma. Chop the bread, including the crust, by hand or in a food processor, taking care not to chop it too fine. The crumbs should be approximately the size of peas. Combine the garlic and oil with the bread crumbs in a small baking dish and bake in a preheated 400° oven until crisp, approximately 10 minutes. Watch the bread crumbs carefully, as they can burn very easily.

Pasta all' Insalata Usticese

WARM PASTA SALAD FROM USTICA

SERVES 4 TO 6

The island of Ustica off the coast of Sicily is famous for its seafood. In the very early hours, before the sun rises, the lights of small fishing boats dot the dark morning sea. Every restaurant and trattoria serves the most amazing fish soups, wonderful sweet lobster, and delicate grilled fish. This is our version of a special dish served to us at Le Campanelle on Ustica during a particularly intense heat wave in late summer.

1 *pound fresh tuna*

½ *cup extra-virgin olive oil, divided*

Juice of ½ lemon

Salt and freshly ground black pepper

Finely chopped fresh red chile pepper to taste

4 *large tomatoes, ripe but firm*

2–3 *tablespoons chopped fresh basil*

2–3 *tablespoons chopped fresh mint*

2 *garlic cloves, peeled and minced*

1 *pound imported penne rigate*

Place the tuna in a glass dish. Drizzle with ¼ cup extra-virgin olive oil and the lemon juice. Let marinate in the refrigerator for several hours. Return to room temperature. In a skillet gently sauté the tuna in the marinade for about 15 minutes, adding salt and pepper, and turning once until just cooked. Cool and break up into large chunks. Chop the tomatoes. Combine the chile pepper, tuna, tomatoes, herbs, garlic, and ¼ cup olive oil, and add salt and pepper to taste. Cook the pasta in abundant boiling salted water until al dente. Drain well and toss with the tuna and tomato mixture. Correct the seasonings and serve immediately.

PASTA FROM THE SEA

Salsa di Tonno al Forno

SHELLS WITH BAKED TOMATO SAUCE AND TUNA

SERVES 4 TO 6

*T*he simplicity of this dish belies its strength. Baking tuna, tomatoes, and anchovies with olive oil produces a dish rich with flavor. The resulting juices are on the thin side, so be sure to cook the pasta just until al dente, so that it can absorb the juices without losing the bite. This dish is also great served as an entree with lots of bread to soak up the *sugo* (sauce). Inspired by Giuliano Bugialli's rendition of the original tomato sauce, circa 1841.

5 *large, red, ripe tomatoes, stems removed*

1 *pound fresh tuna, sliced into ½-inch-thick steaks*

4 *anchovy fillets, drained of oil and rinsed*

Red chile pepper flakes to taste

½ *cup extra-virgin olive oil*

1 *pound imported conchiglie*

Cut the tomatoes crosswise into approximately ½-inch slices. Place a layer of tomatoes in a small ovenproof baking dish. Lay the tuna steaks over the tomatoes and top with the anchovy fillets and red chile pepper flakes. Layer the remaining slices of tomato over the fish and pour the extra-virgin olive oil over all. Bake in a preheated 400° oven for approximately 15–20 minutes or until the fish flakes when pierced with a fork. Before serving, transfer the contents of the baking dish to a pasta serving bowl. Break up the fish with a fork. Cook the pasta in abundant boiling salted water until al dente. Quickly drain and add to the bowl containing the tuna-tomato mixture. Toss the pasta and serve immediately.

Fusilli Lunghi all'Amalfitana
LONG FUSILLI AMALFI STYLE

SERVES 4 TO 6

We enjoyed this pasta dish at a small trattoria in Amalfi right off the coast road. From our window we watched the parade of tour buses making their perilous way along that tortuous road, the air punctuated by the sound of horns honking at every twist and turn. Across the way, steep cliffs plunged down to meet sparkling blue waters, and there were flowers in bloom everywhere — brilliant red geraniums, apricot and fuchsia bougainvillea spilling out of terra-cotta urns, and tender roses. In this recipe the mozzarella becomes tangled in the long strands of fusilli, and its mild flavor contrasts well with the rich essence of the olive paste.

½ cup extra-virgin olive oil, divided

4 anchovies

1½ pounds ripe tomatoes, peeled, seeded, and cut into strips

3 tablespoons black olive paste

1 6½-ounce can tuna, drained

1 pound imported long fusilli

Salt

½ pound fresh mozzarella, cut into small dice

Freshly ground black pepper

1 bunch fresh basil, leaves coarsely chopped

Place ¼ cup extra-virgin olive oil and the anchovies in a large sauté pan. Cook over low heat until the anchovies melt. Add the tomatoes, raise the heat to medium, and cook until the sauce thickens, about 10 to 15 minutes. Combine the olive paste, tuna, and 2 tablespoons of olive oil in a small bowl. Blend well with a fork. Cook the pasta in abundant boiling salted water. When al dente, drain well and place in a heated serving dish. Dress with the remaining olive oil. Add the olive and tuna mixture and toss to coat the pasta. Add the tomato-anchovy sauce and toss. Sprinkle with the mozzarella and basil, toss again, and serve immediately.

Pasta con le Sarde

SERVES 4 TO 6

The look of this dish is pure Sicily, with the saffron-tinted strands of pasta, dark green feathery fennel, pale pine nuts, plump little black raisins, and silvery flashes of sardines. People who think they hate sardines find themselves loving this extraordinary pasta dish. Begin the meal with Sicilian Green Olive Salad and end with Gelo di Melone, both from *Cucina Fresca* (see pages 279 and 252), for a truly Sicilian experience.

1 *pound fresh sardines*

2 *cups wild fennel tops*

1 *medium onion, peeled and finely diced*

½ *cup extra-virgin olive oil*

3 *anchovies*

Salt and freshly ground black pepper to taste

¼ *cup pine nuts, lightly toasted*

2 *tablespoons currants, plumped in warm water for 20 minutes, drained, and patted dry*

Generous pinch of saffron dissolved in 1 cup water, plus extra saffron for pasta bowl

1 *pound imported spaghetti*

Toasted bread crumbs (see page 46)

Scale the sardines, clean them, and remove the central bones and the heads. Cut the sardines into coarse pieces. Cook the fennel greens in abundant boiling salted water until tender, about 10 minutes. Remove the greens with a slotted spoon and drain in a colander, pressing them down with the back of a spoon to remove excess water. Reserve the cooking water. Finely chop the greens.

In a large sauté pan cook the onion in the extra-virgin olive oil over low heat until the onion is limp and transparent. Add the anchovies and stir until they fall apart. Add the sardines to the pan and toss in the onion and oil. Add the chopped fennel, season with salt and pepper, and cook for approximately 5 minutes. Add the pine nuts, currants, and saffron-flavored water. Cook gently until the saffron water reduces by half. Meanwhile, bring the reserved fennel cooking water to a boil. Add the pasta and cook until al dente. Drain the pasta, reserving some of the cooking water, sprinkle with the extra saffron, and toss with the sauce, adding reserved water as needed to create a more liquid consistency. Sprinkle with toasted bread crumbs. Allow the dish to rest for a few minutes before serving. Serve additional bread crumbs on the side.

Pasta al Mediterraneo

The Mediterranean evokes the scent of wine-dark olives, the fragrance of basil, the brilliant splashes of color from huge, coarse-skinned lemons, and the taste of seafood. Tuna is used a great deal in Italy, fresh and *sott'olio* (preserved in olive oil), both considered choice eating. This pasta dish holds up well and can be served several hours later at room temperature, if desired.

12–14	oil-cured black olives, pitted		2	6½-ounce cans tuna, drained
3	tablespoons pine nuts, lightly toasted		1	pound imported perciatelli, broken into 3-inch lengths
1	large garlic clove, peeled and minced			Juice of 1 large lemon
3	tablespoons chopped Italian parsley		6	tablespoons extra-virgin olive oil
1–2	bunches fresh basil, leaves cut into julienne			Salt

Coarsely chop the black olives and the pine nuts separately. In a pasta serving bowl, combine the olives, pine nuts, garlic, parsley, basil, and tuna. Mix gently, breaking up the tuna very slightly. Cook the pasta in abundant salted boiling water until al dente. Drain the pasta well and place it in the serving bowl. Dress with the lemon juice and extra-virgin olive oil. Season with salt and mix well. Serve immediately.

Conchiglie al Sapore di Mare

SEASHELLS-BY-THE-SEA

SERVES 4 TO 6

This dish is made for hot weather. All the preparations can be done in advance except cooking the pasta. Serve with a tart and fragrant chilled white wine.

1½ *pounds squid*

1 *pound medium shrimp, cooked in the shell, peeled*

2 *pounds mussels, cleaned and steamed open, shelled, and juices strained*

4 *large garlic cloves, peeled and lightly crushed*

1 *red bell pepper, roasted, peeled, seeded, and cut into julienne*

¼ *cup small black olives, such as Niçoise or Gaeta*

½ *cup extra-virgin olive oil*

Juice of 1 lemon

Handful fresh basil leaves

Salt and freshly ground black pepper to taste

1 *pound imported conchiglie*

Lemon wedges

To clean fresh squid, carefully pull the head and tentacles from the body sac. Cut the tentacles above the eyes. Pop out the little ball or beak in the center of the tentacles. Discard it and the innards. Pull out the glasslike bone in the body sac and discard. Peel off the skin. Thoroughly rinse the interior of the body sac and the tentacles. Drain. Cut the body sac crosswise into ¼-inch-thick rings. Cook in salted boiling water until tender, about 20 minutes. Drain.

Combine all ingredients in a bowl except the pasta and lemon wedges. Toss well and marinate 1 hour to 24 hours. If marinating the seafood 1 hour, do not refrigerate. If marinating longer, refrigerate the seafood, then allow to return to room temperature before proceeding with the recipe.

Cook the pasta in abundant boiling salted water until al dente. Drain well. Remove the garlic from the seafood mixture and toss with the hot pasta. Correct the seasonings and serve immediately with lemon wedges on the side.

Linguine ai Granchi
LINGUINE WITH CRABMEAT

SERVES 4 TO 6

Threads of pasta and crab intertwine so that each forkful is a delectable mix. Delicious and convenient, this dish can be assembled in advance with only the cooking of the pasta left for the last minute. Find the freshest crab possible. You will ruin the dish if you use frozen crab. It's too watery.

1½ *pounds fresh lump crabmeat*
Juice of 2 lemons
2 *garlic cloves, peeled and minced*
Handful chopped Italian parsley

10 *small fresh basil leaves, coarsely chopped*
½ *cup extra-virgin olive oil*
Salt and freshly ground black pepper to taste
1 *pound imported linguine*

Pick through the crabmeat carefully to remove any shell and cartilage. Place the crabmeat in a small bowl. Add the lemon juice, garlic, parsley, and basil. Stir gently to mix. Add the extra-virgin olive oil, salt, and pepper. Mix well. Set the mixture aside to marinate for at least 1 hour, preferably overnight. Bring the mixture back to room temperature before using and place in a pasta serving bowl. Cook the linguine in abundant boiling salted water until al dente. Drain and toss immediately with the crabmeat mixture in the serving bowl.

Linguine alle Vongole
LINGUINE WITH WHITE CLAM SAUCE

SERVES 4 TO 6

This classic sauce is served in every restaurant and trattoria in Naples where they use very tiny clams called *vongole veraci*. Use only the freshest, smallest clams and cook them only long enough for their shells to open. A small variety of butter clam is now farm-raised here. Ask your fishmonger for them for nothing is less appetizing than a big tough clam. Every time we eat this dish, the table ends up strewn with shells, bread crumbs, and spots of olive oil — a carelessness that is the mark of a casual, unpretentious meal, thoroughly enjoyed.

3 *pounds fresh clams*
Salt
1 *cup extra-virgin olive oil*
6–8 *garlic cloves, peeled and minced*
1 *whole cayenne pepper or 1 teaspoon red chile pepper flakes*

2 *cups dry white wine*
½ *cup chopped Italian parsley*
1 *pound imported linguine*

Place the clams in abundant cold salted water to soak. (The kitchen sink is more convenient than a bowl for this.) The water should be as salty as the sea to convince the clams to relax, open up a little, and give up their last traces of sand. Soak the clams for ½ hour. Lift them out of the water, a few at a time, rinse under cold running water, and place in a bowl. Clean the sink thoroughly of all sand and fill again with cold water and salt. Gently add the clams to the water and let soak for another ½ hour. Lift the clams out of water and rinse under cold water. Place the cleansed clams in a bowl, discarding those that are open and do not close to the touch, any with cracked shells, and any that seem too heavy (they are probably filled with mud).

Heat the extra-virgin olive oil in a large skillet. Add the garlic and cayenne pepper, or red chile pepper flakes, and cook over low heat briefly. Add the clams, dry white wine, and parsley. Cover the pan and turn heat to high. Shake the pan back and forth every couple of minutes. Check the clams after 5 minutes. They are done when the shells are open. Do not overcook them!

Cook the pasta in abundant boiling salted water until al dente. Quickly remove clams from pan. Add cooked pasta to skillet and mix briefly with clam juices over high heat. This allows the pasta to absorb the flavorful clam juices. Place pasta and remaining juices into a shallow serving bowl. Arrange cooked clams in their shells on top of pasta. Serve immediately.

Spaghetti ai Calamari
SPAGHETTI WITH SQUID

SERVES 4 TO 6

The long, slow cooking gives the squid a meltingly tender texture and results in an intensely flavored sauce that is almost a squid stew. This is definitely for squid lovers. Sometimes squid are sold as "cleaned," but actually still require a fair amount of work. This is an important step that must not be overlooked.

1 *pound squid*

¼ *cup extra-virgin olive oil,
plus 1 tablespoon*

1 *small onion, peeled and
chopped*

2 *handfuls chopped Italian
parsley*

3 *garlic cloves, peeled and
chopped*

1 *cup dry red wine*

1 *28-ounce can imported
Italian tomatoes, with
juice*

*Salt and freshly ground
black pepper to taste*

1 *pound imported spaghetti*

To clean fresh squid, carefully pull the head and tentacles from the body sac. Cut the tentacles above the eyes. Pop out the little ball or beak in the center of the tentacles. Discard it and the innards. Pull out the glasslike bone in the body sac and discard. Peel off the skin. Thoroughly rinse the interior of the body sac and the tentacles. Drain. Cut the body sac crosswise into ¼-inch-thick rings. The squid is now ready to be cooked.

Heat ¼ cup extra-virgin olive oil in a heavy-bottomed enamel or stainless steel pot. Add the onion and cook slowly until translucent. Add the parsley, garlic, and the cleaned, drained, and cut-up squid. Sauté briefly until the garlic gives off its aroma, then add the red wine. Cook over high heat until the wine evaporates. Add the tomatoes and their juice, crushing the tomatoes with your fingers as you add them to the pan. Bring the mixture to a simmer over medium heat. Cover the pan and cook over low heat for at least 1½ hours or until the squid is completely tender. Check the sauce periodically for consistency. If it is too liquid, remove the cover the last 15 minutes of cooking to reduce to a thicker sauce. If the sauce is too thick and squid is still tough, add more liquid as necessary during cooking. Add salt and pepper.

Cook the pasta in abundant boiling salted water until al dente. Quickly drain and place in a shallow serving bowl. Toss the pasta with 1 tablespoon extra-virgin olive oil. Add the squid-tomato sauce and mix. Serve immediately.

Fedelini coi Canestrelli

FEDELINI WITH SCALLOPS

Scallops have a sensuously smooth flesh, well suited to pick up the flavor of the herbs in this dish. Cook the scallops lightly, just until they turn opaque, to maintain their unique texture. The juice they release combines with the lemon and olive oil to create the sauce.

1 *pound fresh scallops*
½ *cup extra-virgin olive oil*
2–3 *garlic cloves, peeled and minced*
2 *small dried red chile peppers, crushed*
Small bunch Italian parsley, leaves chopped

3 *sprigs fresh oregano, leaves finely chopped, or ½ teaspoon dried oregano*
Salt and freshly ground black pepper
1 *pound imported fedelini*
Juice of ½ lemon

If using small scallops, cut them in half. If you use large scallops, cut them into ½-inch dice. In a sauté pan combine the extra-virgin olive oil, garlic, and red chile peppers. Sauté over low heat until the garlic is lightly colored. Add the parsley and oregano, and stir for 1 to 2 minutes in the flavored oil. Add the scallops, season with salt and pepper to taste, and cook over high heat until they are just opaque. Meanwhile, cook the fedelini in abundant boiling salted water. Drain when al dente and place in a shallow serving bowl. Toss with the scallop sauce and lemon juice.

Spaghettini alla Rustica
RUSTIC SPAGHETTINI

SERVES 4 TO 6

Inspired by Pasta con le Sarde (see page 174), this dish combines the sweet flavors of shrimp and wild fennel with the more assertive flavors of oregano and red chile pepper. Toasted bread crumbs absorb the sauce and cling to the strands of pasta to help carry the flavor. This is a good rustic pasta, as its name implies. Serve with a cold Sicilian white wine, and follow with big wedges of watermelon.

1 *pound medium shrimp*
½ *cup extra-virgin olive oil*
2 *garlic cloves, peeled and minced*
Crushed dried red chile pepper to taste

2 *cups finely chopped, tender, wild fennel tops*
Pinch of dried oregano
Salt
1 *pound imported spaghettini*
½ *cup toasted bread crumbs (see page 46)*

Clean the shrimp by removing the shells and deveining them. In a large sauté pan combine the extra-virgin olive oil, garlic, and red chile pepper. Sauté for 2 to 3 minutes. Add shrimp, oregano, and salt, and sauté over high heat for about 4 minutes or until shrimp are just opaque. Meanwhile, cook the spaghettini and fennel tops in abundant boiling salted water until pasta is al dente. Quickly drain and toss with the shrimp and flavored oil. Sprinkle with some of the toasted bread crumbs, toss again, and serve with additional bread crumbs on the side.

Linguine e Gamberi all'Erbe
LINGUINE WITH HERBED SHRIMP

SERVES 4 TO 6

*I*nspired by a recipe by noted Italian chef and author Luigi Carnacina, this unusual dish contains an abundance of herbs. Thyme is a welcome companion to the more familiar Italian duet of basil and parsley. The shrimp are cooked separately from the tomatoes to ensure that they do not become overcooked. It takes much longer for tomatoes to thicken into sauce than it does to cook shrimp. This sauce makes an especially savory base for a risotto!

1 *pound medium shrimp, peeled and deveined*

½ *cup extra-virgin olive oil, divided*

Bunch fresh thyme or 1 teaspoon dried thyme

Large handful chopped Italian parsley

1 *large or 2 small bay leaves*

Salt and freshly ground black pepper to taste

3 *garlic cloves, peeled and chopped*

1 *28-ounce can imported Italian tomatoes, drained*

1 *pound imported linguine*

Cook the shrimp in ¼ cup extra-virgin olive oil in a medium saucepan with the thyme, parsley, bay leaves, salt, and pepper. Cook just until the shrimp turns pink and is slightly firm. Do not overcook.

To make the sauce, heat ¼-cup extra-virgin olive oil in a medium saucepan, add the garlic and sauté briefly just until it turns opaque. Add the tomatoes directly to the pan by putting them through the coarse disk of a food mill. Cook the tomatoes quickly over medium heat until the sauce thickens. At this point add the shrimp and all the herbs to the sauce. Heat through so the shrimp are warm but not overcooked.

Cook the pasta in abundant boiling salted water until al dente. Quickly drain and place in a shallow serving bowl. Add the shrimp–tomato sauce and mix. Serve immediately.

PASTA DELLA MACELLERIA

Pasta from the Butcher Shop

*A*lthough we are not big meat eaters, there are times when an autumn or winter chill is in the air and a hearty pasta with a savory ragù is very satisfying.

This chapter includes some fast-cooking meat sauces, such as one with veal, thyme, and cream. You will also find sauces that require longer cooking than any others in the book. Cooking meats slowly with aromatic vegetables is sometimes necessary to tenderize and sweeten the meat. A prime example is Bolognese sauce, which requires about 3 hours of very slow cooking to create the creamy, rich sauce that goes so well with fresh pasta.

Buy the best-quality meat available, preferably meat that comes from grass-fed animals and has no hormones added. It is leaner and purer. When we desire a rich meat-based sauce we go to an old-fashioned butcher shop, which has the highest-quality meats and greatest variety. There is a clean, orderly look to a good butcher shop with its white tile walls and rows of refrigerated counters displaying trays of carefully prepared cuts of meats, all daintily separated by rows of parsley pom poms. The butcher is as much a food craftsman as is a baker of fine breads — an expert who can guide you through the many choices available for any dish you want to prepare.

Serve these pastas with deep-hued red wine, the kind that smells of violets, rich and fragrant to match the flavors of the sauces.

PASTA DELLA MACELLERIA

Salsa Ricca e Espressa

RICH FAST SAUCE

SERVES 4 TO 6

In Campania all parts of the pig are prized, including the fat and skin. Although this sauce ignores the current trends in health and diet, it can be a welcome change. Amazingly, it is less fatty than an all-meat sauce, since you remove the pork skin before serving. Nothing beats this recipe for speed in producing a full-bodied, flavorful sauce.

¼ cup extra-virgin olive oil

1 garlic clove, peeled and minced (optional)

1 28-ounce can imported Italian tomatoes

1 piece pork skin, approximately ¼–½ pound

4–5 fresh basil leaves

Salt and freshly ground black pepper to taste

1 pound penne

Extra-virgin olive oil for drizzling

Heat the extra-virgin olive oil in a deep skillet. Add the optional garlic and cook briefly until it releases its characteristic aroma. Pass the tomatoes, juice and all, through the coarse disk of a food mill directly into the skillet. Add the pork skin and basil. Cook over moderately high heat until the sauce thickens, approximately 20 minutes. Add salt and pepper. Remove the pork skin before serving. Cook the pasta in abundant boiling salted water until al dente. Quickly drain and place in a serving bowl with the tomato sauce. Drizzle a little extra-virgin olive oil over the pasta and mix well with the sauce.

Gnocchetti Rigati con
Pancetta e Fagioli Borlotti

THIN RIGATONI WITH ITALIAN BACON
AND CRANBERRY BEANS

SERVES 4 TO 6

A simple farm-style sauce, combining pancetta, beans, and pasta, that is quick to make yet satisfies as much as any ragù.

¼ cup extra-virgin olive oil

½ onion, peeled and finely diced

1 carrot, peeled and finely chopped

1 stalk celery, finely diced

5 slices pancetta, coarsely chopped

3 garlic cloves, peeled and minced

1 28-ounce can imported Italian tomatoes

1 can borlotti or pinto beans, drained

Salt and freshly ground black pepper to taste

1 pound imported gnocchetti rigati

Freshly grated Parmesan or Pecorino Romano cheese

Heat the extra-virgin olive oil in a large skillet. Add the onion, carrot, and celery, and cook over medium heat, stirring frequently, until the vegetables soften. Add the pancetta and cook over medium-high heat until it gives off its fat. Add the garlic and cook until it gives off its characteristic aroma. Put the tomatoes and all their juice through the coarse disk of a food mill directly into the skillet. Cook over high heat until the tomatoes begin to thicken. Add the beans and continue cooking until sauce thickens, being careful while stirring to keep the beans whole. Add salt and pepper. Cook the pasta in abundant boiling salted water until al dente. Quickly drain and place in a shallow serving bowl. Add tomato-bean mixture and toss carefully. Pass Parmesan or Pecorino Romano cheese.

Rotelle al Vitello

CARTWHEELS WITH VEAL SAUCE

SERVES 4 TO 6

*A*good sauce for a special occasion when time is short. The creamy pink sauce clings to the pasta, while little bits of veal and onion get caught in the spokes of the wheels. And you thought this shape was just for kids!

3 *tablespoons unsalted butter*
½ *small onion, finely diced*
2–3 *sprigs fresh thyme*
¾ *pound freshly ground veal*
Grated rind of 1 lemon
Salt and freshly ground black pepper to taste

4–5 *imported Italian canned tomatoes, seeded and pureed*
1 *cup fresh cream*
1 *pound imported rotelle*
Freshly grated Parmesan cheese

Melt the butter in a medium skillet. Add the onion and thyme, and sauté over low heat until the onion softens. Add the ground veal, lemon rind, salt, and pepper. Sauté until the veal loses its raw color. Add the pureed tomatoes and the cream, and cook over low heat until the sauce thickens. Cook the pasta in abundant salted boiling water until al dente. Drain well. Remove the thyme sprigs from the sauce. Toss the pasta with the sauce and a few tablespoons of Parmesan cheese. Pass additional grated cheese.

Linguine all'Agnello
LINGUINE WITH LAMB SAUCE

SERVES 6 TO 8

*I*n this traditional dish from the Sicilian kitchen of Signora Di Gregorio, the triad of butter, peas, and rosemary creates an indefinable flavor that sends you back for more — and more. The peas are braised along with the lamb and forsake their bright green color on the way, permeating the sauce with their savory sweetness. Serve the Sweet Tomato Sauce (see page 129) on the side so that those who wish can top their servings with a bright splash of sauce.

4 *tablespoons (½ stick) unsalted butter*

¼ *cup extra-virgin olive oil*

1 *onion, peeled and thinly sliced*

1 *garlic clove, peeled and put through a garlic press*

2 *pounds boneless leg of lamb, cut into 1-inch cubes*

2 *sprigs fresh rosemary*

½ *cup white wine*

1 *10-ounce package frozen peas or 2 cups shelled fresh peas*

Salt and freshly ground black pepper to taste

1 *pound imported linguine*

1 *recipe Sweet Tomato Sauce (see page 129)*

Freshly grated Parmesan cheese

Melt the butter and extra-virgin olive oil together in a heavy-bottomed casserole. Add the onion and garlic and slowly fry over moderate heat until onion wilts. Add the lamb and sauté over high heat until well seared on all sides. Add the rosemary and white wine. Adjust the heat to a simmer. Cover the casserole. Cook for 45 minutes or until the lamb is half cooked. Add the peas, salt, and pepper. Cover and continue simmering until the lamb is so tender that it begins to fall apart. The peas should be well cooked.

Cook the linguine in abundant boiling salted water until al dente. Heat Sweet Tomato Sauce and set aside. Drain linguine and place in individual pasta dishes. Pour a generous ladleful of lamb sauce over each serving. Top with a small ladleful of Sweet Tomato Sauce, if desired. Pass Parmesan cheese.

Ragù d'Agnello

LAMB SAUCE

SERVES 4 TO 6

This sauce is from the Abruzzi, a beautiful mountainous region in central Italy bordering on the Adriatic. It is a beautiful area of rugged cliffs, grazing sheep, and gnarled trees set against bright blue water. The Abruzzi is the home of shepherds, so lamb is ubiquitous in the regional cooking. After the initial cooking of the sauce, if any fat separates from the meat tip the pan and pour it off. Lamb and rosemary are naturally paired, both rich and fragrant. Red chile pepper lifts the flavors.

- 3 tablespoons extra-virgin olive oil
- 2 garlic cloves, peeled and minced
- 2 sprigs fresh rosemary
- 3 tablespoons chopped Italian parsley
- ½ teaspoon red chile pepper flakes
- ¾ pound freshly ground lean lamb
- Salt and freshly ground black pepper to taste
- ½ cup dry white wine
- 2 pounds ripe tomatoes, peeled, seeded, and pureed
- 1 pound imported rotelle
- Freshly grated Pecorino Romano cheese

Combine the extra-virgin olive oil, garlic, rosemary sprigs, parsley, and red chile pepper in a large sauté pan. Cook over low heat for several minutes or until the garlic releases its fragrance. Add the lamb and sauté gently until the meat loses its raw color. Season with salt and pepper. Add the wine, raise heat to medium, and cook until the wine evaporates. Add the pureed tomatoes. Cover and cook over medium-low heat until the tomatoes thicken into a sauce, about 20 minutes. Remove the rosemary sprigs. Cook the rotelle in abundant salted boiling water until al dente. Drain well and toss with the sauce. Serve with Pecorino Romano cheese.

Ragù Misto
TOMATO SAUCE OF MANY MEATS

SERVES 6 TO 8

The flavors of the lamb, pork, beef, and veal merge in the slow cooking to produce a deep and mellow sauce that takes well to freezing and reheats beautifully. Some find this ragù is even tastier the second time around, so it's a good sauce to have on hand.

¼ cup extra-virgin olive oil
1 onion, peeled and diced
1 stalk celery, minced
1 carrot, peeled and minced
1 bay leaf
Handful minced Italian parsley
2 garlic cloves, peeled and minced
5 leaves fresh basil, chopped, or 1 teaspoon dried basil

¼ pound each ground lamb, pork, beef, and veal
2 28-ounce cans imported Italian tomatoes, with juice
Salt and freshly ground black pepper to taste
1 pound imported gnocchetti rigati
Freshly grated Parmesan cheese

Heat the extra-virgin olive oil in a large heavy-bottomed casserole. Slowly sauté the onion, celery, carrot, bay leaf, parsley, garlic, and basil until the onion wilts and is nearly translucent. Add the ground meats and fry over high heat until all traces of pink are gone. Puree the tomatoes, with their juice, in a food processor, or pass them through the medium disk of a food mill. Add pureed tomatoes to the meat. Stir and add salt and pepper. Cook over moderate heat at a low simmer for at least 1 hour. Cook the gnocchetti rigati in abundant boiling salted water until al dente. Drain and place in individual pasta bowls. Top each serving with a ladleful of sauce. Pass Parmesan cheese.

Tagliatelle alla Bolognese

SERVES 4 TO 6

Wе had this version of the Emilia-Romagna classic one evening at the home of fashion designer Marina Spadafora. The addition of milk sweetens the sauce and gives it a subtle creamy texture. An unusual feature of the sauce is that the *battuto* of celery, carrots, and onion is not sautéed first, but rather, all the ingredients are added at once. The milk acts as the cooking medium, and the longer the sauce cooks the more the milk sugars develop.

1 *ounce dried porcini mushrooms*

2 *celery stalks, peeled and minced*

2 *carrots, peeled, trimmed, and minced*

1 *onion, peeled and finely diced*

1 *garlic clove, peeled and minced*

2 *pounds ground chuck*

½ *pound sweet Italian sausage*

2 *cups milk*

1 *cup red wine*

2 *tablespoons finely chopped Italian parsley*

2–3 *fresh sage leaves, coarsely chopped*

3–4 *tablespoons imported Italian tomato paste*

2 *cups broth or water, plus additional as needed*

1 *pound fresh fettuccine or 1 recipe Pasta all'Uovo I or II (pages 32–33), cut into fettuccine*

Unsalted butter, softened at room temperature

Freshly grated Parmesan cheese

Put the porcini mushrooms in a small bowl and cover with warm water. Let soak for about 30 minutes. Meanwhile, place the celery, carrots, onion, garlic, meats, milk, wine, herbs, and tomato paste in a large frying pan or medium casserole. Stir with a wooden spoon to mix all the ingredients thoroughly. The milk will make the meat fluffy in texture and help to break it up. Begin to cook over moderate heat. Drain the porcini mushrooms and rinse them to remove any traces of dirt. Chop the mushrooms. Strain the soaking liquid. Add the mushrooms and strained liquid to the sauce. Continue to cook over moderate heat until the meat loses its raw color. Add the broth or water. Simmer the sauce for a minimum of 2½ hours, or until all the flavors come together into a rich, deep-tasting sauce. Add additional broth or water as necessary during the long cooking to keep the sauce liquid. It should not be super-thick. When the sauce is ready, cook the fettuccine in abundant salted boiling water until al dente. Drain well and place in a shallow serving bowl. Add the sauce and softened butter to the pasta and gently toss. Serve with Parmesan on the side.

Sardinian Sausage Sauce

SERVES 4 TO 6

Although this is called a sausage sauce, we prefer to use freshly ground pork. This produces finer results with less fat and fewer extraneous seasonings like fennel. Saffron is the star here, adding its unique exotic flavor. Try to find malloreddus, a traditional Sardinian dry pasta shape made by La Casa del Grana, which has saffron worked into the dough. If unavailable, use cavatelli, and add saffron to the pasta cooking water.

¼ cup extra-virgin olive oil

1 onion, finely diced

2 garlic cloves, peeled and minced

10 fresh basil leaves, chopped, divided

Small handful chopped Italian parsley

½ pound freshly ground pork

½ teaspoon red chile pepper flakes

Generous pinch of saffron

1 28-ounce can imported Italian tomatoes, seeded and pureed

Salt

1 pound malloreddus with saffron worked into the dough, or imported cavatelli

Freshly grated Pecorino Romano cheese

In a large sauté pan combine the extra-virgin olive oil, onion, garlic, half the basil, and all the parsley. Sauté until the onion softens. Add the ground pork, red chile pepper, and saffron, and cook gently until the meat loses its raw color. Add the pureed tomatoes and season with salt. Simmer the sauce until the juices thicken. Cook the malloreddus or cavatelli in abundant boiling salted water until al dente. Drain well and toss with the sauce. Sprinkle with the remaining basil. Serve with Pecorino Romano cheese on the side.

Gnocchetti Rigati con Salsicce
THIN RIGATONI WITH SAUSAGE SAUCE

SERVES 4 TO 6

Gnocchetti rigati is a pasta that is similar in shape to rigatoni but thinner and slightly smaller. We usually prefer to use gnocchetti rigati in recipes that call for rigatoni because during the cooking the larger shape tends to split and flatten on to itself. The gnocchetti stay beautifully round, allowing the sauce to be scooped up into the hollow tube. If you like the look of sausage "coins," cut the sausage into ½-inch circles instead of removing the casings. Kids love it this way!

¼ cup extra-virgin olive oil

½ small onion, peeled and minced

2 garlic cloves, peeled and minced

2 thick slices pancetta, coarsely chopped

4 sweet Italian sausages

1 28-ounce can imported Italian tomatoes

Pinch of red chile pepper flakes

Salt and freshly ground black pepper to taste

2 tablespoons freshly grated Pecorino Romano cheese, plus additional for table use

Small handful chopped Italian parsley

1 pound imported gnocchetti rigati

In a medium skillet, gently cook the onion and garlic in the extra-virgin olive oil until the onion begins to wilt. Remove the sausage meat from the casings and crumble into the skillet. Add the pancetta and cook until no trace of pink remains in the sausage and the pancetta has rendered its fat. Add the tomatoes, lifting them out of the can and crushing them with your fingers as you transfer them to the skillet. Add all the juice from the tomatoes. Add the red chile pepper flakes, salt, and pepper. Stir and cook the sauce over medium heat for at least ½ hour, adding a bit of water if the sauce begins to thicken too much. When the sauce is thick enough to coat a spoon and loses its watery quality, add 2 tablespoons of Pecorino Romano cheese and stir. Cook the pasta in abundant boiling salted water until al dente. Drain and transfer to a heated serving dish. Add the hot sauce and mix thoroughly. Sprinkle a handful of grated cheese over the finished pasta. Top with chopped parsley. Serve immediately, passing additional grated cheese.

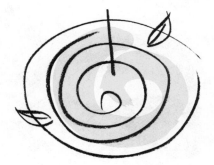

Pasta al Forno e Ripieni

Baked and Stuffed Pasta

Pasta Anna

*T*his chapter differs from the others in that the recipes are longer and more complicated. One advantage is that all the work of preparing the pasta, cooking the sauce, and assembling or stuffing the finished dish can be done well in advance. Some dishes can be made over 2 days, by preparing the sauce a day ahead. Although these dishes require extra time, they are not difficult to make. They just require patience and a love for the tasks at hand. The results are impressive. We usually reserve these special dishes for festive occasions or for long, leisurely Sundays.

The term *pasta al forno* means "pasta from the oven," and encompasses a large category of dishes, including elegant lasagna made with fresh pasta as well as more rustic baked dishes made with dried pasta. For the latter, we choose sturdy shapes that can be cooked twice, first in water, then in the oven when assembled with other ingredients. These peasant dishes are fairly easy to put together. They are best made in earthenware baking dishes that can be brought to the table. Some have beautiful golden crusty surfaces created from cheese or bread-crumb toppings. One magnificent molded dish is lined with eggplant. Another is a tomato stuffed with pasta that has been tossed in mint, parsley, and Pecorino Romano. The lasagna, made with fresh pasta, is simply elegant. One layers the thinnest possible fresh spinach pasta with a creamy mixture of mascarpone and mozzarella.

Because all these dishes can be made in advance they are perfect for feeding a crowd. A warm communal feeling is created when everyone partakes from the same steaming dish. Serve a variety of antipasti first — grilled marinated vegetables, olives flavored with herbs, sliced prosciutto. Bring out the pasta al forno, then serve a big mixed salad of lettuces, raw sliced fennel, and slivers of carrot. Place big bowls of ripe, sweet fruit on the table.

The stuffed-pasta recipes, too, have the convenience of advance preparation. We include cannelloni stuffed with a savory mixture of creamy veal, béchamel, and thyme; an elegant, bright yellow saffron, half-moon pasta filled with veal, as well as homey ravioli with a ricotta and spinach filling. The fillings for these pastas are generally milder than for the baked pastas, so as not to overwhelm the delicate flavor of the fresh pasta. These dishes are especially beautiful because of all their fanciful shapes and colors of the filling peeking through the thin pasta. We love serving them to friends, whose reactions are invariably favorable ones.

Pasta alla Poverella
POOR PASTA

This simple, savory baked pasta dish is set firmly in the tradition of *la cucina povera,* the poor kitchen. It is made with the least expensive, most available ingredients. If it needs a bit more liquid, add some of the water in which the potatoes soaked, probably only ¼ cup or less. An ideal choice for a pot-luck supper or a picnic, it is equally tasty served hot or at room temperature.

½ *pound imported perciatelli or bucatini, broken in half*

Extra-virgin olive oil

3 *potatoes, peeled and thinly sliced, covered with water until needed*

3 *ripe tomatoes, stems removed, sliced*

Salt and freshly ground black pepper to taste

5 *fresh basil leaves, coarsely chopped*

Small handful chopped Italian parsley

¼ *cup freshly grated Pecorino Romano cheese, divided*

¼ *cup freshly grated Parmesan cheese, divided*

Cook the pasta in abundant boiling salted water until almost, but not quite, al dente. Drain well and set aside. Meanwhile, grease a glass or earthenware baking dish with the extra-virgin olive oil. Make a layer of potato slices in the baking pan, then top it with a layer of sliced tomatoes. Add salt and grind some fresh pepper over tomatoes. Add the basil and parsley. Drizzle some extra-virgin olive oil over the tomatoes. Layer all the cooked pasta on top of the tomatoes. Sprinkle half the Pecorino and half the Parmesan on top. Layer the rest of the potatoes and tomatoes over the pasta, finishing with tomatoes. Add more salt and pepper and a drizzle of olive oil. Sprinkle the rest of the grated cheeses over the tomato layer. Cover the baking dish with aluminum foil. Place in a preheated 350° oven for approximately 30 to 40 minutes, or until the potatoes are tender when pierced with the tip of a sharp knife. Remove the foil, raise the heat to 400°, and bake until the cheese on the tomatoes begins to brown. Serve hot or tepid.

Pasta alla Anna

SERVES 6 TO 8

The invention of a good friend, Anna Morra, who decided to combine some of her favorite Neapolitan ingredients, and discovered a truly savory pasta al forno.

1 *pound imported orecchiette*
Extra-virgin olive oil

1 *large eggplant, cut into*
1-inch dice

1 *recipe Rich Fast Sauce (see*
page 189) or Simple
Tomato-Basil Sauce (see
page 128)

1 *pound smoked mozzarella,*
cut into 1-inch dice

Freshly grated Parmesan
cheese

Salt and freshly ground black
pepper to taste

Cook the orecchiette in abundant boiling salted water until al dente. Drain and set aside, adding 1 tablespoon of olive oil to prevent the pasta from sticking together. Pour extra-virgin olive oil into a skillet to a depth of 1½ inches. Heat the oil and fry the diced eggplant over high heat, being careful not to crowd the pan. As the eggplant becomes a deep golden brown, remove from the hot oil with a slotted spoon and drain on paper towels. Oil a 9½ x 12-inch baking dish. In a large bowl mix together the cooked pasta, the sauce, the smoked mozzarella, and a small handful of grated cheese. Add salt and pepper. Add the fried eggplant and gently fold it into the pasta mixture so that it doesn't fall apart. Spoon the pasta-eggplant mixture into the oiled baking dish. Sprinkle a small handful of Parmesan cheese on top. Cover the pan with aluminum foil. Place the dish in a preheated 350° oven. Bake for 40 minutes, then remove foil and turn heat up to 400°. Bake at 400° for 5 to 10 minutes more, or just until the Parmesan cheese begins to brown and the dish is bubbling.

Cannelloni al Vitello

CANNELLONI STUFFED WITH VEAL AND SAUSAGE

SERVES 6 TO 8

A subtle dish with just the touch of creaminess you want for a special dinner with friends or family. Cannelloni are simpler to prepare than you might imagine. They have the advantage that each step can be prepared ahead of time when convenient, and the whole dish can be assembled in advance for baking later in the day.

FOR THE BÉCHAMEL:

3 *tablespoons unsalted butter*

3 *tablespoons all-purpose unbleached flour*

2 *cups milk*

Salt and freshly ground black pepper to taste

FOR THE FILLING:

4 *tablespoons (½ stick unsalted butter)*

2 *tablespoons extra-virgin olive oil*

½ *onion, peeled and minced*

¼ *pound sweet Italian sausage, casings removed*

1 *pound ground veal*

1 *garlic clove, peeled and minced*

Handful chopped Italian parsley

1 *sprig fresh thyme or ¼ teaspoon dried thyme*

2 *ripe tomatoes, peeled, seeded, and coarsely chopped (optional)*

FOR THE CANNELLONI:

1 *cup Sweet Tomato Sauce (see page 129)*

1 *recipe Pasta all'Uovo I (see page 32)*

Freshly grated Parmesan cheese

TO MAKE THE BÉCHAMEL SAUCE:

Melt the butter in a small saucepan over low heat. Add the flour and stir to form a smooth paste. Heat the milk in a separate saucepan. When the milk is hot but not boiling, pour it into the roux (butter-flour mixture), stirring constantly with a whisk or wooden spoon. Cook over low heat until the sauce thickens and the floury taste is gone. Add salt and pepper. Set aside.

TO PREPARE THE FILLING:

Melt the butter with the extra-virgin olive oil in a skillet. Cook the onion over low heat until it becomes translucent and soft. Add the sausage, veal, garlic, parsley, and thyme, and cook over medium heat until the meat loses all traces of pink. Transfer the meat mixture to a bowl. Add 1 cup of béchamel sauce and mix thoroughly. Correct the seasoning. Set aside.

TO PREPARE THE PASTA:

(See page 31 for instructions on making fresh pasta.) Roll out the pasta to the second thinnest setting on the pasta machine. Cut the sheet (*sfoglia*) into 6-inch squares. As you work, keep a damp cloth over the pasta sheets not being used to keep them from drying out. Cook the pasta in abundant boiling salted water until al dente. Quickly drain and either place the pasta in a bowl filled with ice water or run cold water gently over pasta to stop the cooking process.

TO ASSEMBLE THE CANNELLONI:

Butter a baking dish just big enough to hold cannelloni in one layer. Coat the bottom with a thin layer of Sweet Tomato Sauce (see page 129). Drain 1 square of pasta well and lay it on the work counter. Take 2 tablespoons of filling and spread evenly along 1 edge of the square. Carefully roll up the pasta and place in the baking dish seam side up. Continue rolling the cannelloni until all the filling is used. Top the finished cannelloni with the remaining béchamel sauce and then spoon on Sweet Tomato Sauce. Sprinkle a handful of Parmesan cheese over all. Bake in a preheated 350° oven for 30 minutes or until bubbling.

Timballo di Fettuccine

This golden, puffy pasta soufflé is infused with the flavors of fresh herbs and cheese. It's as simple as making a béchamel and beating egg whites. Expect the timballo to collapse a little when you remove it from the oven. For a very pretty presentation, serve with a little pool of Simple Tomato-Basil Sauce (see page 128) on the side.

2 *cups milk*
1 *sprig fresh rosemary*
1 *sprig fresh basil*
1 *sprig fresh thyme*
2 *bay leaves*
3 *tablespoons unsalted butter*
3 *tablespoons all-purpose unbleached flour*
Salt and freshly ground black pepper

1 *cup freshly grated Parmesan cheese*
4 *eggs, separated*
1 *pound fresh fettuccine or 1 recipe Pasta all'Uovo I or II (pages 32–33), cut into fettuccine*
Simple Tomato-Basil Sauce (see page 128) optional

Make a béchamel sauce by heating the milk in a saucepan with the herbs until very hot but not boiling. Turn down heat, but keep hot. In another saucepan melt the butter over medium heat. When the butter is bubbling, add the flour all at once and stir with a wooden spoon to form a smooth paste. Add the hot milk to the flour and butter mixture, straining out the herbs, and stirring constantly. Add salt and pepper. Reduce heat and simmer the sauce gently until it thickens slightly and loses its raw taste, stirring as it cooks. Add the Parmesan cheese. Set aside to cool. Lightly beat the egg yolks and add to the cooled béchamel sauce and stir well. Beat the egg whites until stiff. Meanwhile, cook the fettuccine in abundant boiling salted water. Drain well and add the fettuccine to the egg yolk–béchamel mixture. Fold in the beaten egg whites. Transfer the mixture to a buttered soufflé dish. Place in a preheated 375° oven and bake for 20 to 30 minutes or until golden. Serve with Simple Tomato-Basil Sauce, if desired.

Timballo alla Compá Cosimo

SERVES 6

*I*n the lovely town of Ravello, high above the Amalfi coast, sits the restaurant Compá Cosimo. At this simple trattoria the brother and sister who run it cure their own prosciutto, make their own wine, and pick their garlic young so it is fresh and sweet. Although Ravello has more elegant, chandeliered dining rooms, the food offered there is no more delicious than that at Compá Cosimo. This version of a dish we ate at the trattoria always brings back memories of magical gardens filled with the light fragrance of flowers, tall cypresses, and the umbrella pines that frame vast stretches of twisting coastline.

FOR THE SAUCE:

¼ cup extra-virgin olive oil

2 garlic cloves, peeled and minced

¼ pound pancetta, cut into thin strips

1 28-ounce can imported Italian tomatoes, seeded and pureed

¼ cup finely chopped Italian parsley

2 tablespoons coarsely chopped basil

FOR THE POLPETTINE (SMALL MEAT BALLS):

1 thick slice, fresh country bread, crusts removed

¼ cup milk

1 pound ground veal

¼ cup finely chopped Italian parsley

2 garlic cloves, peeled and minced

1 egg, lightly beaten

Grated peel of ½ lemon

Salt and freshly ground black pepper to taste

Grated nutmeg

All-purpose unbleached flour

¼ cup extra-virgin olive oil

FOR THE TIMBALLO:

1 pound imported rigatoni, or other large, tubular pasta

½ pound fresh mozzarella, cut into small dice

2 hard-cooked eggs, peeled and coarsely chopped

½ pound fresh ricotta

½ cup freshly grated Parmesan cheese

Lightly oiled large, deep rustic baking dish

TO PREPARE THE SAUCE:

Combine the extra-virgin olive oil, garlic, and pancetta in a sauté pan. Cook over a low heat until the pancetta renders its fat, but before it crisps. Add the pureed tomatoes and herbs, and cook over medium heat until the sauce thickens. Set aside.

TO PREPARE THE POLPETTINE:

Soak the bread in the milk. When the bread is completely soaked, squeeze out excess moisture by pressing the bread between your palms. Finely chop the bread. In a medium bowl combine with the veal, parsley, garlic, egg, lemon peel, salt, and pepper. Add a dash of freshly grated nutmeg. Mix gently. Sauté a small amount of the mixture, taste, and correct the seasonings. Flour your hands and a work surface. Form small balls of the mixture about ½ inch in diameter and lightly roll them in the flour. Fry the polpettine in hot extra-virgin olive oil until lightly golden, and drain on paper towels.

TO ASSEMBLE THE TIMBALLO:

Cook the rigatoni in abundant boiling salted water until a shade less than al dente. Drain well. Combine the rigatoni with the tomato sauce, polpettine, mozzarella, eggs, ricotta, and Parmesan cheese. Reserve about 2 tablespoons Parmesan. Put mixture into the prepared baking dish. Sprinkle the top with the remaining grated cheese. Bake in a preheated 400° oven for about 20 minutes, or until heated through and the cheeses have melted. Let stand a few minutes before serving.

Pasta al Forno alla Palermitana

OVEN-BAKED PASTA

SERVES 6

*I*n Palermo, pasta al forno is a staple in shops selling cooked foods. At the central marketplace, we saw big trays of this dish, all golden and crusty, baked and ready to take home for dinner. The chunk we bought never made it home, since it makes equally good eating from a standing position!

6 *tablespoons extra-virgin olive oil*

2 *garlic cloves, peeled and minced*

½ *pound freshly ground veal*

1 *28-ounce can imported Italian tomatoes, seeded and pureed*

1½ *cups fresh peas, or half a 16-ounce package frozen peas*

Handful fresh basil leaves, chopped

Salt and freshly ground black pepper to taste

1 *pound imported anellini*

½ *cup toasted bread crumbs, divided (see page 46)*

1 *pound fresh mozzarella, cut into ½-inch dice*

½ *cup freshly grated Pecorino Romano cheese, plus additional for table use*

Put the extra-virgin olive oil and garlic in a small saucepan. Sauté the garlic until it releases its fragrance. Add the veal and sauté until the meat loses its raw color. Add the pureed tomatoes, peas, basil, salt, and pepper, and cook gently until sauce has thickened slightly. Set aside. Cook the pasta in abundant salted boiling water until very firm to the bite. Drain well. Toss with a little extra-virgin olive oil. Oil a rustic baking dish and coat with half the toasted bread crumbs. In a large bowl combine the pasta, sauce, diced mozzarella, and ½ cup Pecorino Romano cheese. Correct the seasonings. Transfer the sauced pasta to the baking dish and press down the top with the back of a wooden spoon. Sprinkle with the remaining bread crumbs. Bake in a preheated 400° oven for about 20 minutes or until top is golden. Let the dish rest for a few minutes. Cut into squares.

Pasta 'ncasciata

SERVES 4 TO 6

From Sicily, where eggplant is king. The strong flavors and rustic beauty of this molded dish single it out as very special. The sauced pasta, full of mozzarella and salame, is encased in overlapping slices of eggplant that look like the petals of a burnished golden flower. When cooked, cut into wedges to serve but do not expect it to hold together like cake. For this recipe, we are indebted to Ada Boni, whose book on regional Italian food acted as one of our first guides.

2–3 *firm, glossy medium*
eggplants

Salt

Extra-virgin olive oil

1 *large garlic clove, peeled and*
lightly crushed

1 *28-ounce can imported Italian*
tomatoes, seeded and pureed

Freshly ground black pepper
to taste

Handful fresh basil leaves,
coarsely chopped

1 *pound imported tubetti*

2 *ounces good-quality Italian*
salame, diced

¾ *pound fresh mozzarella, cut*
into small dice

1 *cup freshly grated Pecorino*
Romano cheese, plus addi-
tional for table use

3 *hard-cooked eggs, peeled and*
sliced

Slice the eggplants lengthwise, approximately ¼ inch thick. Salt and let drain in colander for about 1 hour. Pat dry with paper towels. Heat the extra-virgin olive oil to measure ½ inch up the side of a large frying pan. When the oil is very hot but not smoking, fry eggplant slices until golden brown on both sides. Fry one layer at a time without crowding the pan. Drain on paper towels. Reserve 3 tablespoons of the oil. Line a large, round baking dish with the eggplant slices, overlapping them slightly. Set aside. Chop any remaining eggplant and set aside. Sauté the garlic in the oil. Add the pureed tomatoes and season with salt and pepper. Cook over medium heat until the sauce thickens, about 15 minutes. Stir in the basil and set aside.

Cook the pasta in a generous amount of salted boiling water. Drain well. In a large bowl, combine the pasta and the tomato sauce. Toss and add the salame, mozzarella, 1 cup Pecorino Romano cheese, and the chopped eggplant. Layer the sliced eggs over the eggplant slices in the baking dish. Top with the pasta mixture and pack it down lightly. Bake in a preheated 400° oven for 20 minutes. Carefully invert onto a serving platter. Blot the surface with paper towels. Cut into wedges. Serve with additional cheese on the side.

Pomodori Ripieni di Fedelini

TOMATOES FILLED WITH THIN PASTA AND HERBS

When big handsome tomatoes are in season, this is a dish to make often. Not only is it an excellent first course, but it is also one of the rare pastas we would recommend serving as a side dish. Make a big batch for a party or as part of a buffet. Delicious served at room temperature. We especially like the touch of fresh mint.

6 *large tomatoes, ripe but firm*
Salt
¼ *pound imported fedelini*
¼ *cup extra-virgin olive oil, plus additional for drizzling*
1 *large garlic clove, peeled and minced*
Small handful chopped fresh mint leaves

Small handful chopped Italian parsley
¼ *cup freshly grated Pecorino Romano cheese, plus additional for topping*
Freshly ground black pepper

Cut off the tops of the tomatoes. Remove the seeds. Cut away the pulp and chop finely. Reserve. Salt well the interiors of the tomatoes and invert tomatoes on paper towels to drain. Cook the fedelini in abundant boiling salted water until al dente. Drain well. Toss with ¼ cup extra-virgin olive oil, garlic, mint, parsley, ¼ cup Pecorino Romano cheese, and chopped tomato pulp. Correct the seasonings, adding salt and pepper to taste. Stuff a little of the flavored pasta into each tomato. Drizzle with olive oil and sprinkle with grated cheese. Lightly oil a baking dish just large enough to contain these. Arrange the tomatoes in the dish and bake on the lower shelf of a preheated 425° oven for 15 minutes or until tomatoes have softened slightly. Serve hot or at room temperature.

Pasta Frittata

OPEN-FACED PASTA OMELET

SERVES 4

*T*his recipe, from *Cucina Fresca,* is the ultimate picnic or brunch food. Each pasta creates its own different mosaic when the frittata is sliced, and the addition of tomato sauce adds an orangey tint to the whole.

6–8 *eggs*
½ *cup freshly grated Parmesan cheese*
Salt and freshly ground black pepper to taste

2 *tablespoons extra-virgin olive oil*
1 *garlic clove, peeled and minced*
2 *cups leftover sauced pasta*

Lightly beat the eggs with the Parmesan cheese, salt, and pepper in a bowl, and set aside. Heat the extra-virgin olive oil in a medium, nonstick oven-proof skillet, and in it sauté the garlic briefly. Add the pasta and heat through. Beat the egg mixture again briefly and pour over the pasta in the skillet. Lower the heat. Cook slowly, stirring frequently, until the eggs have formed small curds and the frittata is firm except for the top. To cook the top, place the skillet under a hot broiler or in a preheated 400° oven until the frittata browns lightly. Remove the skillet from the broiler or oven. Let rest for 1 to 2 minutes. Place a plate over the top of the skillet and invert the frittata onto it. Serve at room temperature, cut into wedges.

Cannelloni ai Zucchini

The classic colors of Italy with its palette of red and white and bits of green. This cannelloni is elegant, yet light and summery.

2 *tablespoons extra-virgin olive oil*

3 *small, firm zucchini, ends removed, finely diced*

3 *garlic cloves, peeled and minced*

Large handful chopped Italian parsley

10 *fresh basil leaves, chopped*

6 *fresh mint leaves, chopped*

Salt and freshly ground black pepper to taste

1 *pound ricotta cheese*

1 *large egg, beaten*

¼ *pound mozzarella packed in water, diced fine*

1 *cup freshly grated Parmesan cheese, divided*

1 *recipe Pasta all'Uovo I (see page 32)*

1 *recipe Sweet Tomato Sauce (see page 129)*

FOR THE FILLING:

Heat the extra-virgin olive oil in a small frying pan. Add the zucchini and garlic, and fry lightly over moderate heat until the zucchini is golden brown. Add the herbs, salt, and pepper at the end of the cooking time. Remove from the heat and cool. In a bowl beat together the ricotta, egg, mozzarella, and ½ cup Parmesan cheese with a wooden spoon, or mix together quickly in a food processor or electric mixer. Stir the zucchini-herb mixture into the cheese mixture and set aside while you prepare the pasta.

TO PREPARE THE PASTA:

Roll out the pasta to the second thinnest setting on the pasta machine. Cut the sheet (*sfoglia*) into 6-inch squares. As you work, keep a damp cloth over the pasta not being used to keep them from drying out. Cook the pasta squares in abundant boiling salted water until al dente. Quickly drain and either place in a bowl filled with ice water or run cold water gently over the cooked pasta. This stops the cooking process and allows you to begin to fill the pasta.

Drain the pasta squares well and lay them on the work counter. Take 2 tablespoons of filling and spread evenly along 1 edge of each cooked pasta square. Carefully roll up the pasta. Continue filling and rolling until all the filling is used. As you finish each roll, place it, seam side up, in a lightly oiled baking dish in which you have put a thin layer of Sweet Tomato Sauce on the bottom. Top the finished cannelloni with the remaining tomato sauce. Sprinkle the rest of the Parmesan cheese over all. Bake in a preheated 350° oven for 30 minutes, or until sauce is bubbling and the cannelloni are heated all the way through.

Pasta con la Carne Capuliata

BAKED PASTA WITH SAVORY MEAT SAUCE

SERVES 4 TO 6

Another warming, rustic dish from Sicily. It makes a meal when followed by a refreshingly bitter salad of escarole or endive. For a fitting end to the meal, dip hard cookies in the last drops of red wine.

¼ cup extra-virgin olive oil, divided

1 medium onion, finely diced

2 garlic cloves, peeled and minced

½ cup minced Italian parsley

Small handful fresh basil leaves, chopped

1 tender carrot, peeled and chopped

1 celery stalk, tough strings removed, chopped

¾ pound freshly ground chuck

½ cup dry red wine

1 28-ounce can Italian tomatoes, seeded and pureed

Salt and freshly ground black pepper

1 pound imported tubetti

½ cup freshly grated Pecorino Romano cheese

½ pound imported caciocavallo or provolone cheese, thinly sliced

Heat 3 tablespoons of the extra-virgin olive oil in a medium stockpot over medium heat. Add the onion, garlic, parsley, basil, carrot, and celery. Turn the heat to low and sauté ingredients until they are tender. Add the ground chuck and sauté until the meat loses its raw color. Pour in the wine, turn the heat to high, and cook until the wine evaporates. Add the pureed tomatoes, and season with salt and pepper to taste. Cover and simmer over low heat for about 1 hour. Check occasionally and add water, 3 or 4 tablespoons at a time, as the sauce reduces. Cook the pasta in abundant boiling salted water. Drain the pasta when cooked but still very firm, and toss with the sauce and the Pecorino Romano cheese. Lightly oil a rustic baking dish with the remaining 1 tablespoon olive oil. Alternate layers of sauced pasta with layers of the thinly sliced caciocavallo or provolone cheese, ending with a cheese layer. Bake in a preheated 350° oven for 20 minutes or until cheese melts. Let settle for a few minutes before serving.

Ravioli al Magro
LENTEN RAVIOLI

SERVES 6 TO 8

The most frequently served of all the ravioli and probably the most satisfying, these are delicious with either Simple Tomato–Basil Sauce (page 128) or Sweet Tomato Sauce (page 129) or with melted butter and sage.

1 *bunch fresh spinach or Swiss chard*

½ *pound ricotta, drained*

1 *egg, beaten*

½ *cup freshly grated Parmesan cheese, plus additional for table use*

Salt and freshly ground black pepper to taste

Pinch of nutmeg

1 *recipe Pasta all 'Uovo I (see page 32)*

TO MAKE THE FILLING:

Remove the stalks and stems of the spinach, and carefully wash the leaves in at least 2 changes of water. Place the washed spinach in a small saucepan. Cover and cook over low heat until the spinach wilts. Let cool, then carefully squeeze out liquid from the spinach, using the palms of your hands. Chop finely. Place chopped spinach in a small mixing bowl and add the ricotta, egg, ½ cup Parmesan cheese, salt, pepper, and nutmeg. Mix well with a spoon. Set aside while preparing the pasta.

TO MAKE THE RAVIOLI:

Using a pasta machine, roll out the dough on the thinnest setting, cutting it into sheets of manageable length, approximately 16 inches. Do not roll out too many sheets at a time or the dough will begin to dry out and become difficult to handle. Make a row of generous teaspoons of filling, 1 inch apart, across the center of 1 pasta sheet. Carefully fold the sheet in half toward you, matching the horizontal edges of the dough. Gently press the filling down with your fingertips. Press the dough down between each teaspoon of filling to enclose it. Using a pasta cutter, trim off the edges of the dough and cut apart the ravioli. Gently crimp the edges of the ravioli with a fork. Lay the ravioli on a lightly floured bedsheet or tea towels. Let dry at least 5 minutes before cooking.

TO COOK THE RAVIOLI:

Bring a large pot of salted water to the boil. Add ravioli to the boiling water. Very fresh pasta takes about 2 to 5 minutes to cook. Carefully drain the ravioli and transfer to a warm serving platter. Top with the sauce of your choice. Pass Parmesan cheese.

Ravioli di Melanzane
EGGPLANT-STUFFED RAVIOLI

SERVES 6 TO 8

A textural delight, combining fresh ricotta, soft creamy eggplant, and crunchy toasted walnuts, enveloped in tender folds of fresh pasta.

1 *pound ricotta*

1 *large egg, beaten*

Small handful freshly grated Pecorino Romano cheese

2 *tablespoons walnuts, toasted and diced*

8 *fresh basil leaves, minced, or ½ teaspoon dried basil*

Salt and freshly ground black pepper to taste

Extra-virgin olive oil for frying

1 *eggplant, stem and blossom ends removed, cut into ½-inch dice*

1 *recipe Pasta all'Uovo I (see page 32)*

Sweet Tomato Sauce (see page 129)

Freshly grated Parmesan cheese

TO MAKE THE FILLING:

Using a hand mixer or a food processor with a steel blade, beat together the ricotta, egg, and Pecorino Romano cheese until blended but not super smooth. With a wooden spoon, stir in the walnuts, basil, salt, and pepper. Set aside. Pour the extra-virgin olive oil to a depth of ½ inch in a large frying pan. Heat over high heat and fry the eggplant a little at a time until a deep golden brown. As it cooks, remove the eggplant from the pan with a slotted spoon and place on paper towels to drain. When the eggplant cools, add it to the ricotta mixture, stirring carefully so as not to break up the soft pieces of fried eggplant.

TO MAKE THE RAVIOLI:

Using a pasta machine, roll out the dough on the thinnest setting, and cut it into sheets of manageable length, approximately 16 inches. Do not roll out too many sheets at a time or the dough will begin to dry out and become difficult to handle. Make a row of generous teaspoons of filling, 1 inch apart, across the center of 1 pasta sheet. Carefully fold the sheet in half toward you, matching up the horizontal edges of the dough. Gently press the filling down with your fingertips. Press the dough down between each teaspoon of filling to enclose it. Using a pasta cutter, trim off the edges of the dough and cut apart the ravioli. Gently crimp the edges of the ravioli with a fork. Lay the ravioli on a lightly floured bedsheet or tea towels. Let dry at least 5 minutes before cooking.

TO COOK THE RAVIOLI:

Bring a large pot of salted water to the boil. Add the ravioli to the boiling water. Very fresh pasta takes about 2 to 5 minutes to cook. Ravioli are ready when pasta is tender. Carefully drain the ravioli and transfer to a warm serving platter. Serve with hot Sweet Tomato Sauce. Pass Parmesan cheese.

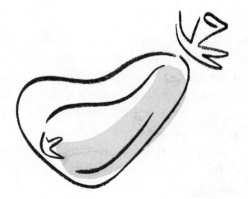

PASTA AL FORNO E RIPIENI

Mezzaluna alla Zafferano
SAFFRON-SCENTED HALF-MOONS

Inspired by the mingling of flavors in the traditional Milanese osso buco, this elegant orangey-gold pasta makes a delicious starter to a formal, multicourse dinner.

8 tablespoons (1 stick) unsalted butter, divided

2 tablespoons extra-virgin olive oil

½ small onion, minced

1 small carrot, peeled and minced

1 small stalk celery, minced

1 garlic clove, peeled and minced

½ pound veal stew meat

½ cup dry white wine

14 ounces imported Italian tomatoes (half 28-ounce can), pureed through food mill

1 bay leaf

2 tablespoons coarsely chopped Italian parsley

1 small strip lemon zest, ½-inch by 2 inches

Pinch of saffron threads, soaked in ½ cup warm water

Salt and freshly ground black pepper to taste

1 egg yolk

¼ cup freshly grated Parmesan cheese, plus additional for table use

1 recipe Pasta allo Zafferano (see page 34)

FOR THE GREMOLATA:

Small handful chopped Italian parsley

2 garlic cloves, peeled and minced

Very finely grated zest of 2 lemons

BAKED AND STUFFED PASTA

TO MAKE THE FILLING:

Melt half the butter and the extra-virgin olive oil together in a casserole or a large, heavy, high-sided skillet. Add the onion, carrot, celery, and garlic, and sauté over low heat until the vegetables wilt and the onion is translucent. Add the veal and brown over high heat. When the meat is thoroughly seared on all sides, add the white wine and deglaze the pan. Add the pureed tomatoes, bay leaf, parsley, lemon zest, 1 tablespoon of the saffron soaking water, salt, and pepper. Cover the pan and braise the meat over a low flame until it is tender, approximately 1 hour. When the meat is tender, remove from the pan, reserving sauce. Finely chop the meat with a knife, or pulse in a food processor until it is minced but not pureed. Place the minced meat in a small mixing bowl. Add the egg yolk, ¼ cup Parmesan cheese, and enough of the reserved sauce to just moisten the mixture. Set aside while you prepare the pasta.

TO PREPARE THE PASTA:

Roll out the prepared Pasta allo Zafferano, as directed on page 37, passing the sheets of dough through the rollers, each time moving them to a thinner setting, until you reach the thinnest setting possible. Remember to keep the sheets of dough covered with a damp cloth as you work to prevent them from drying out too quickly. Using a 4-inch-diameter biscuit cutter, cut out rounds from the thin sheets of pasta. Place 1 teaspoon of the meat filling in the center of each pasta round. Dampen half the edge of the round with water and fold it in half, enclosing the filling in a half-moon shape. Continue until all the filling is used. You should have approximately 55 pieces.

TO PREPARE THE GREMOLATA:

Mix together the parsley, garlic, and lemon zest. Set aside to use as a garnish for the finished dish.

Place the half-moons in abundant boiling salted water and cook just until done. It should take about 2 or 3 minutes, depending on how dry the pasta has become. Meanwhile, melt the remaining 4 tablespoons butter in a small skillet. Drain the half-moons well and place in individual serving dishes. Pour a little melted butter on each serving. Top with 1 teaspoon saffron water, then with 2 tablespoons of the reserved sauce. Sprinkle a bit of the gremolata over all. Serve immediately. Pass Parmesan cheese.

Tortelli di Patate
POTATO-STUFFED RAVIOLI

SERVES 6 TO 8

Signora Nena, the *portiera* of a close friend's apartment house in Milan, comes from Parma. These ravioli are her version of a traditional Parma treat in which grated Parmesan cheese is used with abandon. Do not skimp!

2 large potatoes, peeled

2 slices pancetta, finely chopped

½ pound ricotta, drained

1 cup freshly grated Parmesan cheese, plus additional for table use

Salt and freshly ground black pepper to taste

1 recipe Pasta all'Uovo I (see page 32)

Ragù Misto (see page 195)

TO MAKE THE FILLING:

Place the potatoes in cold salted water and bring to a boil. Turn the heat down to a lively simmer and let the potatoes cook until they are tender when pierced with a fork. Meanwhile, sauté the pancetta in a small skillet until it renders its fat and is cooked but not crisp. Drain the pancetta on paper towels and set aside. When the potatoes are cooked, drain them and mash with a potato masher or put them through a ricer. In a small bowl mix together the mashed potatoes, ricotta, 1 cup Parmesan cheese, salt, pepper, and pancetta.

TO ASSEMBLE THE TORTELLI:

Using a pasta machine, roll out the dough on the thinnest setting, cutting it into sheets of manageable length, approximately 16 inches. Do not roll out too many sheets at a time or the dough will begin to dry out and become difficult to handle. Make a row of generous teaspoons of filling, 1 inch apart, across the center of 1 pasta sheet. Carefully fold the sheet in half toward you, matching the horizontal edges of the dough. Gently press the filling down with your fingertips. Press the dough down between each teaspoon of filling to enclose it. Using a pasta cutter, trim off the edges of the dough and cut apart the separate tortelli. Gently crimp the edges of the tortelli with a fork. Lay the tortelli on a lightly floured bedsheet or tea towels. Let dry at least 5 minutes before cooking.

TO COOK THE TORTELLI:

Bring a large pot of salted water to the boil. Add the tortelli to the boiling water. Very fresh pasta takes about 2 to 5 minutes to cook. Carefully drain the tortelli and transfer to a warm serving platter, layering the pasta with handfuls of grated cheese and hot Ragù Misto.

Triangoli di Pesce

FISH TRIANGLES

SERVES 4 TO 6

In this filling, fresh fish is lightly cooked, gently flaked, and combined with chopped tender Swiss chard, basil, and parsley. Very different from fish mousse fillings found in Frenchified stuffed pastas that have a completely smooth texture made airy by the addition of whipped cream. It is a lean and fresh combination of flavors and textures.

1 *pound fresh firm-fleshed fish fillet (red snapper or halibut)*

2 *tablespoons extra-virgin olive oil*

Salt and freshly ground black pepper to taste

1 *bunch Swiss chard, washed, stems and stalks removed*

⅓ *cup freshly grated Parmesan cheese*

6 *fresh basil leaves, finely chopped*

Small handful chopped Italian parsley

1 *recipe Pasta all'Uovo I (see page 32)*

Olio Santo (see page 95)

TO MAKE THE FILLING:

Coat the fish fillet with the extra-virgin olive oil, salt, and pepper, and bake in a preheated 350° oven until cooked, approximately 7 minutes. Let the fish cool, then flake it apart with your fingertips. Meanwhile, place the washed chard in a small saucepan. Cover and cook over low heat until the chard wilts. Let the chard cool, then carefully squeeze out the liquid with the palms of your hands. Chop the chard finely and place in a small mixing bowl with the Parmesan cheese, basil, parsley, and flaked fish. Add salt and pepper to taste.

TO MAKE THE TRIANGLES:

Roll the prepared Pasta all'Uovo I dough, as directed on page 37, passing the sheets of dough through the rollers, each time moving them to a thinner setting. Roll out the dough, using the thinnest setting possible. Remember to keep the sheets of dough covered with a damp cloth as you work to prevent them from drying out too quickly. Using a fluted pastry cutter, cut the pasta sheets into 4-inch squares.

Place a pasta square on your work surface so that it is turned to look like a diamond. Place 1 kitchen teaspoonful of the fish filling in the center of each square. Dampen 2 adjacent edges of the pasta square. Enclose the filling by folding the square, creating a triangle shape. Continue until all the filling is used.

TO COOK THE TRIANGLES:

Bring a large pot of salted water to the boil. Add the triangles to boiling water. Very fresh pasta takes about 2 to 5 minutes to cook. Carefully drain the triangles and transfer them to a warm serving platter. Serve in individual pasta dishes and drizzle with Olio Santo.

Casonsei di Zucchini e Funghi
PASTA FIRECRACKERS WITH ZUCCHINI AND MUSHROOMS

Casonsei are a traditional Bergamasco specialty filled with meat. We love the shape and decided to try them with a savory yet lighter filling. The pasta shapes are very large, so you need only 3 to 4 per serving.

8 *tablespoons (1 stick) unsalted butter*

1 *tablespoon extra-virgin olive oil*

½ *onion, peeled and minced*

2 *garlic cloves, peeled and minced*

5 *small, firm zucchini, trimmed and cut into ¼-inch dice*

1 *pound fresh mushrooms, trimmed and cut into ¼-inch dice*

3 *sprigs fresh thyme, leaves only*

6 *fresh basil leaves, cut into julienne*

Salt and freshly ground black pepper to taste

½ *pound ricotta*

1 *egg, beaten*

½ *cup freshly grated Parmesan cheese*

1 *recipe Pasta all'Uovo I (see page 32)*

½ *pound (2 sticks) unsalted butter*

1 *bunch fresh sage, leaves only*

TO MAKE THE FILLING:

Melt the butter and extra-virgin olive oil together in a large skillet. Add the onion and cook over low heat until it is translucent. Add the garlic, zucchini, mushrooms, thyme, basil, salt, and pepper, and cook over high heat until the zucchini and mushrooms begin to turn golden. Remove from the heat and scrape the mixture into a medium bowl. When the zucchini mixture is at room temperature, add the ricotta, egg, and Parmesan cheese. Stir well and taste for additional salt and pepper.

TO MAKE THE CASONSEI:

Roll the prepared Pasta all'Uovo I dough, as directed on page 37, passing the sheets of dough through the rollers, each time moving them to a thinner setting. Roll out the dough, using the thinnest setting possible. Remember to keep the sheets of dough covered with a damp cloth as you work to prevent them from drying out too quickly. Using a sharp knife, cut the pasta sheets into rectangles, 4 by 5½ inches.

Place a pasta rectangle on your work surface so that the shorter side faces you. Place 1 heaping tablespoon of the zucchini-ricotta filling in the middle of the pasta square, being careful to leave a ½-inch border on either vertical, longer side. Dampen the pasta close to the zucchini-ricotta filling and enclose the filling by folding the rectangle in half. The dough should be sealed close to the filling, leaving the 1 inch of extra pasta free-falling and unsealed. When the pasta is cooked, this unsealed portion is soft and pretty, like a piece of fabric. Continue this process until all the filling is used.

TO COOK THE CASONSEI:

Bring a large pot of salted water to the boil. Add casonsei to boiling water. Very fresh pasta takes about 2 to 5 minutes to cook. Remove the casonsei with a slotted spoon and drain thoroughly by letting the spoon rest for a few seconds on an absorbent kitchen towel. Transfer pasta to warmed individual pasta dishes. Melt the butter over medium heat together with the sage leaves. Pour over pasta and serve.

Ravioli con Pesto di Olive

RAVIOLI STUFFED WITH RICOTTA AND BLACK OLIVE PASTE

SERVES 6 TO 8

1 *pound fresh ricotta*

1 *egg, beaten*

⅓ *cup black olive paste*

1 *recipe Pasta all'Uovo I (see page 32)*

6 *tablespoons unsalted butter*

Handful fresh basil leaves, cut into thin julienne

Freshly grated Parmesan cheese

TO MAKE THE FILLING:

Combine the ricotta, egg, and olive paste in a bowl and stir until well mixed.

TO MAKE THE RAVIOLI:

Using a pasta machine, roll out dough on the thinnest setting, cutting the dough into sheets of manageable length, approximately 16 inches. Do not roll out too many sheets at a time or the dough will begin to dry out and become difficult to handle. Make a row of generous teaspoons of filling,

1 inch apart, across the center of one pasta sheet. Carefully fold the sheet in half toward you, matching the horizontal edges of the dough. Gently press the filling down with your fingertips. Press the dough down between each teaspoon of filling to enclose it. Using a pasta cutter, trim off the edges of the dough and cut apart the separate ravioli. Gently crimp the edges of the ravioli with a fork. Lay the ravioli on a lightly floured bedsheet or tea towels. Let dry at least 5 minutes before cooking.

TO COOK THE RAVIOLI:

Bring a large pot of salted water to the boil. Add the ravioli to the boiling water. Very fresh pasta takes about 2 to 5 minutes to cook. Carefully drain the ravioli and transfer to a warm serving platter. Drizzle melted butter over the ravioli. Top with basil julienne. Pass Parmesan cheese.

Lasagna Verde al Mascarpone
GREEN LASAGNA WITH ITALIAN CREAM CHEESE

SERVES 6 TO 8

The mascarpone adds its characteristic light richness to this creamy, sweet lasagna.

- 6 tablespoons unsalted butter
- ¼ cup all-purpose unbleached flour
- 3 cups milk
- Salt and freshly ground black pepper to taste
- ½ pound mascarpone
- 1 pound ricotta
- 2 eggs
- 1 recipe Sweet Tomato Sauce (see page 128)
- 1½ cups grated Parmesan cheese
- 1 recipe Pasta Verde (see page 34)

TO MAKE THE BÉCHAMEL:

Melt the butter in a small saucepan over low heat. Add the flour and stir to form a smooth paste. Heat the milk in a separate saucepan. When it is hot but not boiling, pour it into the roux (butter-flour mixture), stirring constantly with a whisk or a wooden spoon. Cook over low heat until the sauce thickens and the floury taste is gone. Add salt and pepper. Set aside. The béchamel should be on the thin side.

In a small bowl combine the mascarpone, ricotta, eggs, salt, and pepper. Mix well. Set aside.

TO MAKE THE LASAGNA:

Roll the prepared Pasta Verde dough, as directed on page 37, passing the sheets of dough through the rollers, each time moving them to a thinner setting. Roll out the dough, using the thinnest setting possible. Cut the pasta sheets into rectangles 4½ by 11 inches. Let the pasta dry while you bring the water to a boil. Briefly cook the lasagna in abundant boiling salted water for just a few seconds. Remember that the pasta will cook again in the oven and you do not want to cook it completely this first time. Lift the pasta out of the boiling water with a Chinese strainer or slotted spoon, and place in a bowl of cold water to stop the cooking process. Lift the lasagna out of the water and place it on kitchen towels to drain.

TO ASSEMBLE THE DISH:

Spread a ladleful of Sweet Tomato Sauce on the bottom of a baking dish. Make a layer of lasagna noodles. Spoon a ladleful of béchamel sauce onto the lasagna. Using a rubber spatula, spread the béchamel evenly. Spoon a ladleful of the tomato sauce over the béchamel. Using a rubber spatula, distribute the tomato sauce over the béchamel. It does not need to be a perfectly even layer. Sprinkle a bit of the grated Parmesan cheese over the tomato sauce. Make another layer of lasagna noodles. Using a rubber spatula, spread half of the mascarpone-ricotta mixture over the lasagna. Spoon a ladleful of the tomato sauce evenly over the mascarpone-ricotta mixture. Sprinkle more Parmesan cheese over the tomato sauce. Continue assembling the dish by adding another layer of lasagna with béchamel and tomato sauce, then a final layer of lasagna, mascarpone-ricotta mixture, and tomato sauce, sprinkling a bit of Parmesan cheese over each layer. You should end with a layer of tomato sauce and Parmesan cheese. Cover the baking dish with aluminum foil and place in a preheated 375° oven for approximately 30 minutes or until lasagna is bubbling hot. Remove foil for last 10 minutes of cooking.

GNOCCHI

Little Dumplings

*J*ust as nearly every culture has its burrito, so it has its dumplings. Whether the dumplings are formed from a simple paste of flour and water, or made of spinach, cheese, and flour, or of potato and flour, the combination of ingredients is usually mixed with flour as a binder, then the dumplings are gently simmered in salted water until done. In Italy dumplings are called gnocchi and are traditionally made with potato or ricotta. We have included a sampling of different kinds. The ones made with ricotta are often called gnocchetti. We also feature one baked gnocchi dish made with semolina flour and polenta. Gnocchi range from the very delicate and light, such as the ricotta gnocchi, with a summery tomato-basil sauce, to the more substantial potato gnocchi served with meat sauce, ideal for removing the chill from a winter day.

Making gnocchi is like making fresh pasta — the procedure is simple yet difficult to explain in words. If an opportunity arises to watch an experienced gnocchi maker at work, do not miss it! It takes trial and error to understand the proper consistency of the dough. It must be soft yet not wet. The best way to learn is to plunge ahead. During your first attempts, have a small pan of simmering water ready so that as you work the dough, you can cook several test gnocchi.

We find that Italian potatoes tend to be drier and more floury than American potatoes; they are easier to handle and the results are consistently good. The very best potato to use here is a yellow Finnish variety now available in some supermarkets and produce shops. These potatoes have the same floury consistency as the Italian and have a smooth, sweet, buttery taste. If Finnish potatoes are unavailable, use a combination of russet for texture and red new potatoes, for taste.

Some cooks insist that eggs have no place in potato gnocchi. We believe it is a matter of personal taste. Gnocchi made without eggs are feather-light and melt in the mouth. The addition of an egg acts as a binder so that the finished product cooks up firmer, more al dente, a quality we like very much.

Gnocchi di Patate

POTATO DUMPLINGS

SERVES 6 TO 8

The best gnocchi we ever tasted were made by an eighty-five-year-old grandmother, Signora Moriconi. We spent time with her in her ancestral home in a tiny village in Amatrice and we watched her expert hands turn simple ingredients into a mountain of light yet firm dumplings, drowned in a savory sauce. Gnocchi are very delicate and do not take to too much mixing to distribute sauce. Signora Moriconi solves the problem by layering the gnocchi with cheese and sauce, thus keeping them whole. These simple gnocchi are also delicious served with a creamy Gorgonzola sauce (see page 116).

2 *pounds yellow Finnish potatoes or 1 pound each russet potatoes and red potatoes*

1 *egg, beaten*

1–2 *cups all-purpose unbleached flour, divided*

Ragù Misto (see page 195)

Freshly grated Parmesan cheese

Place whole, unpeeled potates in cold water to cover. If you use russet and red potatoes, cook them separately. Bring the water to a boil over high heat and continue cooking potatoes until they are tender. Test only 1 potato for doneness, and do not test too often, for each time it is pierced it absorbs more water. When the potatoes are tender, drain and peel them. Put the potatoes through a ricer, mixing both red and russet together at this point, and place the riced potatoes in a medium mixing bowl until cool enough to handle. Add the egg and 1 cup of the flour. Use your hands to mix in the egg and flour, kneading as you would a bread dough but as little as possible, because too much mixing will toughen the gnocchi. The batter should be soft yet hold its shape when the gnocchi are formed. Add more flour, up to 2 cups if necessary (the amount depends on the humidity and on the type and age of the potatoes).

To form the gnocchi, break off pieces as big as a child's fist. With floured hands, gently roll the dough into cylinders about ¾ inch in diameter. Lay the cylinders on a floured board and, using a sharp knife, cut off pieces the width of a finger. Lay the finished gnocchi on a well-floured board or tray, taking care to keep the dumplings separate to prevent their sticking together. Let dry at least 10 minutes.

Bring a large pot of salted water to the boil. Turn the heat down so that the water simmers, and gently drop the gnocchi into the simmering water. Gnocchi are done when they float to the surface. Meanwhile, heat Ragù Misto until bubbling hot, and warm a serving bowl in a low oven. Remove the gnocchi from the simmering water with a slotted spoon and drain thoroughly by letting the spoon rest for a few seconds on an absorbent kitchen towel. Place the drained gnocchi in the serving bowl, in which you have placed a ladleful of Ragù Misto. Make a layer of gnocchi, top with a handful of Parmesan cheese, then a ladleful of sauce. Continue layering in this manner until all the gnocchi are used, ending with a top layer of sauce. Pass additional grated cheese.

Gnocchi di Spinaci
SPINACH-POTATO DUMPLINGS

Spinach gnocchi have a rich flavor and a lovely green color. We prefer to top them with melted butter, fresh sage, and a sprinkling of grated cheese rather than masking them with a tomato sauce.

- 1 *10-ounce package frozen chopped spinach*
- 1 *tablespoon extra-virgin olive oil*
- 2 *small garlic cloves, peeled and minced*
- 2 *pounds yellow Finnish potatoes or 1 pound each russet and red potatoes*

- 1 *egg, beaten*
- 1–2 *cups all-purpose unbleached flour, divided*
- 8 *tablespoons (1 stick) unsalted butter*
- 15 *fresh sage leaves*
  Freshly grated Parmesan cheese

Cook the spinach according to the package directions, using as little water as possible. After the spinach is cooked, drain and let cool. Squeeze as much water as possible out of the spinach. Heat the extra-virgin olive oil in a small frying pan. Cook the garlic and spinach in the oil just a couple of minutes, for flavor and to kill the raw taste of the garlic. Let cool. Place whole, unpeeled potatoes in cold water to cover. If using russet and red potatoes, cook them separately. Bring the water to boil over high heat and continue to cook the potatoes until they are tender. Test only 1 potato for doneness, and do not test too often, for each time the potato is pierced it absorbs more water. When the potatoes are tender, drain and peel them. Pass the potatoes through a ricer, mixing both red and russet together at this point, and place riced potatoes in a large mixing bowl until cool enough to handle. Puree the spinach in a food processor with a steel blade, or chop very finely. Mix spinach together with the riced potatoes in a large mixing bowl, and turn out onto a floured board. Add the egg and 1 cup of the flour. Using your hands, knead as you would a bread dough but as little as possible, for too much mixing will toughen the gnocchi. The gnocchi batter should be soft yet hold its shape when dumplings are formed. Add more flour, up to 2 cups if necessary (the amount depends on the humidity, and on the type and age of the potatoes).

To form the gnocchi, scoop up 1 kitchen teaspoonful of gnocchi mixture and gently roll with floured hands into an oval shape. Bring a large pot of salted water to the boil. Turn the heat down so that the water barely simmers. Gently drop the gnocchi into the simmering water. Gnocchi are done when they float to the surface. Remove the gnocchi with a slotted spoon, drain thoroughly by letting the spoon rest for a few seconds on an absorbent kitchen towel. Gently place in a warm serving bowl. Melt the butter over medium heat together with the fresh sage leaves. Pour bubbling hot melted butter and sage leaves over gnocchi. Garnish with Parmesan cheese.

Gnocchi di Carote
CARROT-AMARETTI DUMPLINGS

*I*t took a friend with a sweet tooth to have the courage to order these special gnocchi at Ciovassino, a restaurant in the Brera section of Milan. We were delighted to find that the sweetness of the amaretti was not overpowering; it was just enough to bring out the flavor of the fresh tomato sauce. If you prefer, top the dumplings with melted butter and sage. To best appreciate the deep orange color of these gnocchi, serve in simple white bowls.

2 *medium russet potatoes*

2 *pounds carrots, peeled, trimmed, and cut into 2-inch pieces*

5 *Amaretti di Saronno cookies*

¾–1 *cup all-purpose unbleached flour*

2 *eggs, beaten*

½ *cup freshly grated Parmesan cheese, plus additional for table use*

Salt and freshly ground black pepper to taste

Simple Tomato-Basil Sauce (see page 128)

Place whole, unpeeled potatoes in cold water to cover. Bring the water to a boil over high heat and continue to cook the potatoes until they are tender. Test only 1 potato for doneness, and do not test too often, for each time the potato is pierced it absorbs more water. When the potatoes are tender, drain and peel them. Put the potatoes through a ricer. Set aside until cool enough to handle. Steam the carrots until very tender. Puree the carrots in a food processor with a steel blade or in a blender. Scrape out the carrot puree and place in a colander to cool and to drain off any excess water.

Grind the amaretti cookies finely, either in a food processor with a steel blade, or by laying the cookies between two sheets of wax paper and crushing them with a rolling pin. In a large mixing bowl mix together the cooled riced potatoes, carrot puree, ground amaretti cookies, flour, eggs, ½ cup Parmesan cheese, salt, and pepper. The mixture will be soft but stiff enough to hold its shape when formed. Bring a large pot of salted water to the boil. Turn the heat down so that the water barely simmers.

To form the gnocchi, either take small rounded teaspoonfuls of carrot-potato batter and push them gently into the simmering water with another teaspoon, or use a pastry bag with a serrated #6 tip. Fill bag with the gnocchi mixture. Hold the bag over a large pot of simmering salted water and carefully push the batter through the tip, cutting it off so that pieces approximately 1½ inches long fall into the water. The gnocchi are done when they float to the surface. Remove the gnocchi with a slotted spoon and drain thoroughly by letting the spoon rest for a few seconds on an absorbent kitchen towel. Serve with Sweet Tomato Sauce. Pass Parmesan cheese.

Gnocchetti di Verdura e Ricotta
DUMPLINGS OF GREENS AND RICOTTA

These light dumplings are relatives of the Tuscan ravioli nudi, "naked ravioli," traditionally made only with spinach. Red chard and arugola add a peppery depth of flavor. For consistent results, it is important to squeeze the greens as dry as possible and to drain the ricotta so that the mixture will not be too wet.

- 1 *bunch each red chard and spinach, washed, stems and stalks removed*
- 2–3 *bunches arugola, washed, stems trimmed*
- 3 *eggs, lightly beaten*
- ¾ *cup freshly grated Pecorino Romano cheese*
- ¾ *cup freshly grated Parmesan cheese, plus additional for table use*
- 1 *pound ricotta, drained*
- *Salt and freshly ground black pepper to taste*
- 1 *cup all-purpose unbleached flour*
- *Simple Tomato-Basil Sauce (see page 128)*

Cook the greens in the water that clings to their leaves after being washed. When the greens are tender, drain and cool. Squeeze them between the palms of your hands until they are dry. Chop the greens finely. Combine them with the eggs, grated cheeses, ricotta, salt, and pepper, and mix well. Spread the flour on a work surface. Form the ricotta mixture into balls about ¾ inch in diameter. Roll lightly in flour. Cook the gnocchi, a few at a time, in abundant boiling salted water. They are ready when they rise to the surface. Lift the gnocchi out with a slotted spoon and drain thoroughly by letting the spoon rest for a few seconds on an absorbent kitchen towel. Serve hot, ladling a few tablespoons of Simple Tomato-Basil Sauce over each serving, with a little Parmesan cheese over the top.

Gnocchetti di Zucchini
ZUCCHINI-RICOTTA DUMPLINGS

The potential combinations of vegetable puree and ricotta are endless for this style of gnocchi. The zucchini add a sweet, light, buttery flavor, perfect for a summer lunch.

- 4 small zucchini, ends trimmed
- 3 garlic cloves, peeled and minced
- 10 fresh basil leaves
- 1¼ pounds ricotta, drained
- 1 cup freshly grated Parmesan cheese, plus additional for the table
- Salt and freshly ground black pepper to taste
- 2½ cups flour, approximately
- 8 tablespoons (1 stick) unsalted butter
- 15 fresh sage leaves

Steam the zucchini with the garlic and basil until tender, then puree in a food processor with a steel blade. In a small bowl mix together the zucchini-garlic puree, ricotta, and 1 cup Parmesan cheese until smooth. Add salt and pepper. Add 1 cup of flour and mix with a wooden spoon, continuing to add flour ½ cup at a time. Begin to knead lightly with your hands as the batter becomes a dough. Add enough flour to create a soft dough that holds its shape when cooked.

To form the gnocchetti, take 1 kitchen teaspoonful of dough and gently roll with floured hands to an oval shape. Bring a large pot of salted water to the boil. Turn the heat down so that the water barely simmers. Drop the gnocchetti gently into the simmering water. They will be done when they float to the surface. Remove the gnocchetti from the simmering water with a slotted spoon and drain thoroughly by letting the spoon rest for a few seconds on an absorbent kitchen towel. Place on a warm serving platter. Melt the butter over medium heat together with the fresh sage leaves. Pour bubbling hot melted butter and sage leaves over the gnocchetti. Garnish with Parmesan cheese.

Gnocchi alla Romana con Polenta
BAKED SEMOLINA AND POLENTA GNOCCHI

SERVES 4 TO 6

These baked gnocchi are in the Roman style. The addition of polenta is not traditional, but adds a delicious taste and beautiful yellow color. Be sure to use coarse-grained semolina, not the finely ground flour used for making pasta.

1 *quart milk*
8 *tablespoons (1 stick) unsalted butter, plus 3 tablespoons, divided*
Salt and freshly ground black pepper to taste
Pinch of nutmeg

¾ *cup polenta or coarse-grained corn meal*
¾ *cup coarse semolina*
2 *cups freshly grated Parmesan cheese, divided*
2 *large egg yolks*

Heat the milk in a medium saucepan with 8 tablespoons butter, salt, pepper, and nutmeg. When the butter is completely melted and the milk just comes to the boil, lower heat and slowly add the polenta and semolina in a continuous rain of grains while you stir constantly. Always stir in the same direction. Cook over low heat for approximately 5 minutes or until the mass begins to pull away from the sides of the pan as you stir. Remove the saucepan from the heat and stir vigorously. Add 1 cup Parmesan cheese and continue stirring. Add egg yolks and mix well.

Rinse a jelly roll pan with cold water and shake it to remove most of the water droplets. You want the baking pan to be moist, so don't dry it. Using a rubber spatula, remove the gnocchi mixture from the saucepan and spread it evenly onto the jelly roll pan to a thickness of approximately ½ inch. Set the gnocchi mixture aside. Melt the remaining butter in a small pan. Using a pastry brush, spread the melted butter evenly onto the gnocchi mixture. Sprinkle the remaining Parmesan cheese evenly on top of the buttered gnocchi mixture. Lightly cover the gnocchi mixture with plastic wrap and refrigerate for at least 1 hour.

Lightly butter a Pyrex baking dish. Remove the gnocchi mixture from the refrigerator and cut out rounds using a 2-inch biscuit cutter. Place the rounds in the buttered baking dish in rows, overlapping them slightly. Take the bits of gnocchi mixture that remain after cutting out the rounds, cut them into diamond shapes and bake them separately in another pan. They are fun to use as a garnish for simple grilled or roasted meats. Place the gnocchi in a preheated 400° oven for approximately 25 minutes or until they are golden brown and bubbling.

BIBLIOGRAPHY

Alberini, Massimo, and Giorgio Mistretta. *Guide all'Italia Gastronomica*. Milano: Touring Club Italiano, 1984.

Alessi, Gabriella. *Cucina di Campagna*. Florence: Bonechi, 1985.

Artusi, Pellegrino. *La Scienza in Cucina e L'Arte di Mangiar Bene*. Florence: Marzacco, 1959.

Benci, Marietta. *Le Ricette della Mia Cucina Fiorentina e Toscana*. Florence: Del Riccio, 1977.

Benini, Zenone. *La Cucina di Casa Mia*. Florence: Olimpia, 1975.

Boni, Ada. *Il Talismano della Felicità*. Rome: Casa Editrice Colombo, 1983.

————. *Italian Regional Cooking*. New York: Bonanza Books, 1969.

Bugialli, Giuliano. *The Fine Art of Italian Cooking*. New York: Times Books, 1977.

————. *Giuliano Bugialli's Classic Techniques of Italian Cooking*. New York: Simon and Schuster, 1982.

Carnacina, Luigi. *Il Carnacina*. Milan: Aldo Garzanti Editore, 1961.

————, and Luigi Veronelli. *La Cucina Rustica Regionale/Italia Meridionale*. Milan: Rizzoli, 1966.

David, Elizabeth. *Classics: Mediterranean Food, French Country Cooking, Summer Cooking*. New York: Alfred Knopf, 1980.

————. *Italian Food*. London: Penguin, 1976.

De Crescenzo, Luciano. *Frijenno Magnanno*. Naples: Edizioni Tursport, 1977.

DiStefano, Bianca. *Cucina Che Vai, Natura Che Trovi*. Palermo: Edikronos, 1981.

Hazan, Marcella. *The Classic Italian Cookbook*. New York: Alfred Knopf, 1976.

————. *More Classic Italian Cooking*. New York: Alfred Knopf, 1978.

Kummer, Corby. "Pasta," *The Atlantic,* July 1986, pp. 35–47.

Lodato, Nuccia. *Le Ricette della Mia Cucina Siciliana*. Florence: Edizioni del Riccio, 1978.

Martini, Anna. *The Mondadori Regional Italian Cook Book*. Milan: Mondadori, 1982.

Molteni, Angela. *Ricettario di Cucina Povera*. Milan: Gammalibri, 1984.

Pepe, Antonietta. *Le Ricette della Mia Cucina Pugliese*. Florence: Edizioni del Riccio, 1977.

Prezzolini, Giuseppe. *Spaghetti Dinner*. New York: Abelard-Schuman, Inc., 1955.

Root, Waverly. *Food*. New York: Simon and Schuster, 1980.

————. *The Best of Italian Cooking*. New York: Grosset and Dunlap, 1974.

————. *The Food of Italy*. New York: Random House, 1971.

————. *Herbs and Spices*. New York: McGraw-Hill, 1980.

Sassu, Antonio. *La Vera Cucina in Sardegna*. Rome: Anthropos, 1983.

Tropea, Ivana. *Le Ricette della Mia Cucina Romana*. Florence: Edizioni del Riccio, 1977.

Zaffina, Giovanna. *Le Ricette della Mia Cucina Calabrese*. Florence: Edizioni del Riccio, 1977.

Zucchi, Linda, ed. *La Cucina Italiana di Casa Nostra*. Florence: Edizioni del Riccio, 1979.

La Cucina Italiana, a monthly magazine, founded 1929.

INDEX

INDEX

267

INDEX

INDEX